NAVAL

Shōkaku-Class Aircraft Carriers

In the Imperial Japanese Navy during World War II

HANS LENGERER AND LARS AHLBERG

Library of Congress Control Number: 2022944551

Cover design by Justin Watkinson
Type set in Impact/Minion Pro/Univers LT Std

ISBN: 978-0-7643-6651-2
Printed in India

Published by Schiffer Publishing, Ltd.
4880 Lower Valley Road
Atglen, PA 19310
Phone: (610) 593-1777; Fax: (610) 593-2002
Email: Info@schifferbooks.com
Web: www.schifferbooks.com

For our complete selection of fine books on this and related subjects, please visit our website at www.schifferbooks.com. You may also write for a free catalog.

Acknowledgments

In compiling this brief history of the Shōkaku-class aircraft carriers, we are indebted to the following individuals who for a long time have given invaluable help in our research of the Imperial Japanese Navy: Messrs. Endō Akira, Fujita Takashi, Hayashi Yoshikazu, Ishibashi Takao, Itani Jirō, Iwasaki Yutaka, Izumi Kōzō, Kamakura Takumi, Kimata Jirō, Kitagawa Ken'ichi, Kitamura Kunio, Koike Naohiko, Maejima Hajime, Mizutani Kiyotaka, Morino Tetsuo, Naitō Hatsuho (via Itani), Nakagawa Tsutomu, Takagi Hiroshi, Takahashi Shigeo, Takasu Kōichi, Tamura Toshio, Todaka Kazushige, Tsuda Fumio, and Tsukamoto Hideki.

Special thanks go to Messrs. Wilhelm Besch and Michael Wünschmann for drawings.

Contents

CHAPTER 1

Introduction

Auspicious cranes flying in the clouds" depicts the etymology of "Zuikaku." A wind blowing over the Himalayas far away. Sunset with peony flowers in full bloom. A dancer flipping her hem. Eastern moon. A crane that flew from here without being invited by the moonlight. Cranes dance, celestial maidens dance, people dance . . . "Zuikaku" means "Auspicious Crane" and "*Shōkaku*" means "Soaring Crane." *Gakken*

The aircraft carriers of the Shōkaku class are generally regarded as being the most successful carriers designed by the Imperial Japanese Navy. They became operational just prior to the Pearl Harbor attack, and their operational records are impressive. Even by the US Navy these carriers were rated highly, and of the US carriers only USS *Enterprise* can match the operational record of *Zuikaku*.

Unfortunately, space does not permit us to deal with these aircraft carriers in great detail. Therefore, emphasis has been put on the outline description of the characteristic features of this class—position of the island bridge, "detonation gas expansion holes" in the upper hangar walls, underwater and horizontal protection, damage control, and machinery—but brief data about the construction, general arrangement, the flight deck, and a few other items such as armament are also presented. This arrangement does not cause any remarkable deficiency, because reference to the volume *Sōryū, Hiryū, and Unryū-Class Aircraft Carriers* in this series can be made.

The operational history is limited to a synopsis of the operations they participated in. *Zuikaku*'s actions in the Battle for the Leyte Gulf[1] in October 1944, which also meant the loss of the last aircraft carrier that had participated in the Pearl Harbor attack, are included in the form of a partial translation of her "Detailed action record" (DAR). It is thought that this is the first time that it is published in English. Due to space limitations, large parts had to be omitted, however, and there are also, unfortunately, some "blanks" and question marks.

A Short Retrospective

On the basis of the recognition that seaplane-carrying warships could not operate their planes under bad weather conditions, the demand for warships that could operate wheeled aircraft, take off and land on the ships, and attack targets on the sea or on the ground beyond the range of any other weapons became urgently necessary. Once more, the Imperial Japanese Navy (IJN), which had performed the first wartime operation of a seaplane-carrying warship in World War I (*Wakamiya Maru* during the conquest of the German colony Tsingtao in 1914) and had experienced the imminent defect of this type in maneuvers thereafter, followed the example of its longtime mentor—the Royal Navy—and built the *Hōshō*, the first ship originally designed to operate wheeled aircraft, later designated an aircraft carrier (CV).

The fighting power of this new type of warship was recognized to be so overwhelming that even before the completion of the *Hōshō*, qualitative and quantitative restrictions of this type—the only one aside from capital ships—were included in the Washington Arms Limitation Treaty (concluded in February 1922) and were continued with the First London Arms Limitation Treaty (concluded in April 1930). While in the first treaty *Hōshō* had been recognized as a trial ship and was consequently placed outside the restrictions, the second treaty canceled this possibility, and *Hōshō* was included into the quantitative total limitation of 81,000 tons of aircraft carriers.

Like the US Navy, the IJN had also made use of Article IX of the Washington Treaty and had converted the battle cruiser *Akagi* and the battleship *Kaga* into aircraft carriers by using the maximum possible tonnage (actually exceeding the permitted tonnage of 27,000 tons per ship by approximately 3,000 tons). Therefore, this revision limited the IJN's available tonnage of aircraft carriers—a disadvantage Japan had tried to evade by building the small *Ryūjō* as a trial aircraft carrier of the smallest possible tonnage for a fleet carrier, because of the official policy to maintain numerical equality with the US Navy—still more and resulted in deficiencies in the design of the medium-sized *Sōryū*. Her deficiencies could, however, fortunately be expunged, at least to a considerable degree,[2] in her quasi sister

Shōkaku and *Zuikaku* formed the 5th Carrier Division (*Dai 5 Kōkū Sentai*), and they are here seen during training in October–November 1941. The training schedule for this newly formed carrier division was very intense. It is said that almost every day, planes were lost or damaged and that a number of planes even crashed into the island structure. Accidents also occurred during ship-to-ship refueling drills. All these accidents caused the 5th Carrier Division to be regarded as being below the standard of the 1st and 2nd Carrier Divisions. *Kure Maritime Museum*

Hiryū, as mentioned in this series' previous volume, *Sōryū, Hiryū, and Unryū-Class Aircraft Carriers*. Considerable influence hereupon had also been exerted by the *Tomozuru* and the Fourth Fleet incidents in 1934 and 1935, respectively, by which extremely important factors, such as stability and hull strength calculations, had to be greatly revised. Therefore, the design philosophy of the IJN's warships changed from Captain (later, rear admiral) Fujimoto Kikuo's progressive designs to more-conservative designs. Fujimoto tried to get rid of the traditional design concepts of his predecessor, Vice Admiral Hiraga Yuzuru, but because Fujimoto's successor, Captain (later, vice admiral) Fukuda Keiji, was a pupil of Hiraga and was also supported by him, a return to more-traditional designs was made.

Learning from the errors in earlier designs, caused by incorrect stability and strength calculations and seriously evaluating the experiences gained when constructing the previous aircraft carriers, the Japanese designers made every effort to avoid repetitions in the future ships, which were no longer limited by treaty restrictions.

Building the Armament Responding to the Strategic Maxim

The "Washington system" was discontinued on December 31, 1936, and the IJN decided to build the fleet thought to best fulfill its particular strategy—to end a short war by a decisive fleet battle à la Tsushima between the main forces of the opponents and the stages prior to the battle—the attrition and the interception operations. For these the value of the aircraft carrier and its only attack weapon—the aircraft[3]—gradually grew up more and more. With budget restrictions also relaxed, the planners in the Naval General Staff (NGS) decided requirements for the two aircraft carriers included in the first naval building program after the termination of the qualitative and quantitative restrictions,[4] by which they were to distinguish themselves by an excellent design, considering especially stability and strength, and also strong armament, efficient propulsion system, long endurance, improved habitability, easy maintenance of aircraft, etc.

In other words, the principle of the "superiority of the single ship" (*kokan yūetsu*), adopted because of the 60 percent ratio compared with the 100 percent of the Royal Navy and the US Navy in the "Washington system," should be continued and further improved, because even the "hawks" had recognized that numerical equality with the US Navy could not be obtained irrespective of the official building policy, and the possession of ten aircraft carriers aspired to in the force structure of the third revision of Japan's national defense guidelines, as the three parts of Japan's national defense policy can be recognized, in June 1936.[5]

CHAPTER 2

Requirement of the Naval General Staff

To attain individual superiority, the planners of the Naval General Staff shifted to the large-sized aircraft carrier type and required the following properties:

Aircraft	
Fighter type 0 ("Zero")	18/2
Dive-bomber type 99 ("Val")	27/5
Torpedo bomber type 97 ("Kate")	27/5
Total	72/12 = 84[6]
The reserve planes shall be stored in the hangar not fully dismantled in order to be quickly operable. This condition has to be considered when deciding the hangar area, because considerable space is needed for the reserve planes.	
Aircraft weapons shall consist of 90 800 kg bombs, 306 250 kg bombs, and 540 60 kg bombs. 496 tons of aviation gasoline shall be stored.	

Speed and Endurance	
34.5 knots, 18 knots	10,000 nm
Antiaircraft armament	
Type 89 40 cal. 12.7 cm HAG	16 (8 twin mounts)
Type 96 25 mm MG 36	(12 triple mounts)

Protection	
Magazines	Against 800 kg bombs released from level bombers (3,000 m altitude) and against 8" (20.32 cm) shells fired from distances between 12,000 and 20,000 m
Machinery spaces	Against 250 kg bombs released from dive-bombers and against 12.7 cm shells

These requirements make it clear that the Naval General Staff wished to incorporate all the experience gained in the design, construction, and operation of the earlier carriers. The number of aircraft of the original requirement corresponded to the capacity of *Akagi* and *Kaga* (91 and 90, respectively) after conversion; speed was the same as *Sōryū* and *Hiryū*, while endurance was superior to any of these four carriers. The antiaircraft armament was similar to *Kaga* as rebuilt, and protection against bombs, shells, and torpedoes was significantly improved compared with *Sōryū* and *Hiryū*. With their large aircraft capacity, high speed, good endurance, heavy antiaircraft armament, and strong protection, the new carriers were, in theory, an advance in every operational respect on their predecessors. It remained only for the design engineers of the Basic Design Section of the Navy Technical Department (NTD) to be able to realize the staff requirements.

CHAPTER 3

Change of the Basic Design Due to the Relocation of the Island Bridge

The aircraft carrier design team, headed by Lieutenant Commander (later rear admiral) Yagasaki Masatsune, created an enlarged, structurally and generally improved version of *Hiryū*, with the position of the island bridge also to port and at approximately half the length. In response to the requirement for reinforced protection, the designers adopted a new formula with regard to the underwater protection, strengthened the horizontal protection, and also tried to minimize damage within the hangars by fitting "expansion" or "blowing-out" holes in the hangar sides. The total area of the hangars had to be increased, not the least because of the Naval General Staff's requirement of reserve planes. The requirement for speed and endurance was fulfilled by machinery developing not only the maximum power of a plant fitted in an IJN warship—namely, 160,000 shp—but also having the necessary flexibility for quick maneuvering, so necessary in case of being attacked from the air. The fitting of an auxiliary rudder beside the main rudder should guarantee steering to some degree. The dimensions of the hull enabled the designers to place high-angle guns (HAGs) and machine guns (MGs) at positions giving greatest possible arcs of fire.

With an apparently complete response to the Naval General Staff's requirements the construction of the *Shōkaku* started in the Yokosuka Arsenal in December 1937 and was followed by *Zuikaku* in the Kawasaki Kōbe Shipyard in May 1938. However, the design had to be revised during the construction because the Navy Air Department (NAD) had changed its opinion to place the island bridge to port and at almost half the length, as in *Akagi*, to the arrangement adopted for *Kaga* and *Sōryū*. The hasty redesigning was begun at the end of 1938 and was approved by the Navy Technical Department Technical Conference on February 13, 1939, after details had been discussed in the No. 3 Committee on the seventh; the report was submitted to the navy minister on March 27, and the revision was authorized. Rear Admiral Fukuda Keiji, then chief of the Basic Design Section, made a rather long statement about the reasons for the change of the design. The following items are drawn from the minutes of the said conference.

The reason for placing the bridge amidships in *Akagi* and *Hiryū* was to meet the request of the Navy Air Department to increase the length of deck available for takeoff. The Navy Air Department explained that the aft half of the flight deck was sufficiently long for landing on, but for takeoff the bridge became an obstruction when located approximately one-third of the flight deck's length from the bow, where the planes had not yet gained sufficient speed, and turbulence around the bridge affected their steering. If the bridge was located amidships it facilitated the preparation of the aircraft for takeoff and was also preferable if aircraft were landed over the bow. However, positioning the bridge amidships brought it too close to the exhaust uptakes on the starboard side; it therefore needed to be relocated to port. From a stability point of view, the portside position was advantageous because the weight of the bridge and the uptakes canceled one another out. This design was discussed in the Navy Technical Department Technical Conference with the agreement of the Navy Air Department, and experiments were then conducted to determine the effect on airflow over the flight deck and the streaming of smoke.

Before the fitting-out of *Akagi*, a wooden mockup of the bridge was placed in the intended position, and the carrier sailed from Yokosuka to Sasebo to measure the airflow over the deck, and to test the impact on the takeoff and landing of aircraft and the steering of the ship. The conclusions drawn from the experiments give the impression that the decision to locate the island amidships and to port on *Akagi* and *Hiryū* was made on the basis of inconclusive results in testing. It was stated that "the influence on airflow over the deck could not be investigated sufficiently(!), but the position of the bridge did not pose a problem for landings"; it was further stated that "from the viewpoint of steering of the ship, it is preferable to have the bridge in the fore part of the ship . . . and it is proposed to compensate for the poor visibility forward by an auxiliary bridge."

However, after construction of the new carriers had already begun, negative opinions regarding the arrangement of the bridge of *Akagi* and *Hiryū* were expressed; the view was advanced that airflow over the flight deck on these two ships had a negative effect on takeoff and landing operations compared to *Kaga*. There was also concern about the shorter landing area, which could become a serious problem as future aircraft increased in size and had higher landing speeds.

In the autumn of 1938, the Navy Air Department and Navy Technical Department addressed the issue of whether the construction of the Shōkaku class should proceed in accordance with the original design, or whether the position of the bridge should be changed to starboard. In October and November 1938, 451 test landings and takeoffs were made from the flight deck of *Akagi*.[7] The landings were filmed to provide a basis for discussion, and the airflow over the deck was made visible by the generation of steam at the bow. The conclusions took into account day and night landings with the wind from various directions and resulted in a decision to change the position of the bridge on the Shōkaku class to that of *Kaga* and *Sōryū*, the sole proviso being that this revision should "not . . . have a significant influence on the completion dates."

The redesign had to be undertaken in a hurry because of this proviso and required a degree of improvisation and compromise. Because of the advanced state of the construction of *Shōkaku*, the relocation of the supporting structure for the bridge inside the hangars and most of the ventilation ducts from port to starboard would have caused construction delays, so they were left as originally designed. The result was a reduction in the hangar area for the forward section of the upper hangar, which was made narrower to accommodate the supporting structure for the new island (the number of aircraft that could be stowed in the hangar decreased by one); however, it was expected that this loss of hangar area could be compensated for by a change in the way the aircraft were stowed.[8] The flight deck was extended 1 m on the port side, and the width outboard of the island to starboard was reduced to 0.5 m in order to rebalance weights, and the change also involved the fitting of 100 metric tons of ballast on the port side, which increased trial displacement to 29,800 metric tons. It was also calculated that maximum speed would be reduced from 34.2 knots to 34.0 knots—this fear proved to be groundless, and both ships were slightly faster—and radius from 10,000 nautical miles to 9,700 miles at 18 knots. Other consequences were the shortening of the takeoff deck to 72 m (accepted by the Navy Air Department, and a marked improvement in visibility forward from the compass platform reduction of the "dead" zone from 200 m to 170 m). The items most discussed at the Navy Technical Department Technical Conference were the reduction in the firing arcs of some high-angle guns and machine guns and their fire control systems because of the new bridge arrangement, but little could be done beyond relocating some of the searchlights and their controls.

CHAPTER 4

Construction

The most-significant events were the work in connection to the redesign, for which there was close cooperation among the main personnel responsible in the Navy Technical Department, the Yokosuka Arsenal, and the Kawasaki Shipyard—and the acceleration of the construction of *Zuikaku* because of the probable outbreak of the war; her scheduled building period was some four months shorter than that of sister *Shōkaku*, in the event that the completion dates had to be put back for both ships early in 1941 due to the late delivery of key items of the propulsion plant (boilers, main engines, and most of the auxiliary machinery). However, once these materials were delivered, the completion date was advanced in preparation for war, and no delay was permitted.

Table 1: Building Data and Fate

	Builder	Laid down	Launched	Completed	Fate	Removed from list
Shōkaku (No. 3)	Yokosuka Arsenal (*Kōshō*)	December 12, 1937	June 1, 1939	August 8, 1941	Sunk June 19, 1944, by USS *Cavalla* (SS-244) in position 11°50'N, 137°57'E (140 nautical miles N of Yap Island)	August 31, 1945
Zuikaku (No. 4)	Kawasaki Heavy Industries Warship Works (*Jūkōgyō Kansen Kōjō*), Kōbe	May 25, 1938	November 27, 1939	September 25, 1941	Sunk October 25, 1944, by US carrier-based aircraft in position 19°20'N, 125°20'E (220 nautical miles ENE of Cape Engaño)	August 31, 1945

Shōkaku was laid down at Yokosuka Arsenal (*Kōshō*), no. 2 slipway, on December 12, 1937, less than a month after the aircraft carrier *Hiryū* had been launched. The *Shintō* rites during the laying-down ceremony were performed by a *Shintō* priest, and he is here performing the purification (*shūbatsu*) ritual. The officer on the far right of the attendees is presumed to be Admiral Hyakutake Gengo, then commander of the Yokosuka Naval District. *Sekai no Kansen*

Taken on February 20, 1938, this photo shows the condition of *Shōkaku* two months after the laying-down ceremony. Looking from starboard aft, the huge keel (the "backbone" of the construction) is clearly visible because the progress of work at the stern is less progressed. The explanation in Japanese (ommited) says, *from top to bottom:* "Condition of construction progress 4.8%. Date of photo February 20, 1938. Weight of worked material 1,255 tons, 738 kg. Number of rivets 57,158." The height of the frames to which the outer hull bottom plates were fixed was also the height of the double bottom, because the plates of the inner hull bottom were also fixed to them. The building on the left side of the hull is the 1st Plate Shop *(Dai 1 Tōtetsu-Jō)*, where the shaping of the structural members (such as bending, flanging, straightening, punching, drilling, etc. of the steel plates, using heavy presses and rolls) was done.

Progress of work on *Shōkaku*'s hull on April 20, 1938. The hull is now 6.6% complete and the weight has increased to 2,063.585 tons, and the number of rivets is more than quadrupled and now numbers 262,709. The bow is at the upper edge of the photo. The outer-hull bottom plates are fixed to the frames, and the fitting of the inner-hull bottom plates is underway. Note the connection between the longitudinals and the frames. The number of rivets indicates that riveting was still the principal method used, because the application of electric welding of strength members had been prohibited following the investigation of the Fourth Fleet incident.

The condition on January 20, 1939. The bow is on the upper edge, and the photo was taken from the position of the gantry crane. The huge rectangular opening in the lower hangar deck is for the forward aircraft elevator. Below is the elevator pit, where later the motors, winches, etc. for operating the elevator are to be placed. Forward of the opening, the deck plating has progressed. Note the concave shape of the foremost frames to port, indicating the gradual increase of the flare toward the bow. The carrier is now 44.8% complete, the weight is 12,345.602 tons, and the number of rivets is 2,244,424.

Shōkaku almost ready for launching on May 30, 1939, at 16:00. She was the first warship in the IJN fitted with a bulbous bow, and the fitting of this type of bow was a result of investigations made during the design of the battleships of the Yamato class, but *Shōkaku*'s bulb was considerably smaller than Yamato's. Only the lower part of the ship is shown, because this is a memorial photo of the main responsible naval architects and naval engineers in charge of the design and construction. For reason of secrecy, the draft markings were not painted in white Roman numerals, as was customary. Instead they painted I, Ro, Ha, etc. in Japanese, using black color, but it was doubted if it was useful, since the spacing was identical.

First row, from left: Engineer Tachikawa Yoshiharu (main responsible for the hull), engineer Ogura Takeo (main responsible for machinery and fitting out), Technical Lieutenant Commander Saitū Kanjirō (responsible for the hull), Technical Commander Inagawa Seiichi (main responsible for the design), Captain Ezaki Iwakichi (chief of the shipbuilding division), Technical Commander Nishimura Yahei (responsible for main turbines and main responsible for launching), Technical Commander Fukui Matasuke (main responsible for fitting-out), Technical Commander Hirohata Masuya (main responsible for investigations)

Second row, from left: Technical Sublieutenant Nakagawa Katsuya (fitting-out), Technical Sublieutenant Matsushita Kiyosaku (hull), Technical Lieutenant Morooka Atsushi (fitting-out), Technical Lieutenant Commander Koyama Katsu (design), Technical Lieutenant Commander Maeda Tatsuo (chief of fitting-out), engineer Masuda Chiyoji (design), Technical Lieutenant Harada Shin'ichirō (design)

Third row, from left: Technical Sublieutenant Fukui Shizuo (hull), Technical Sublieutenant Niwa Seiichi (inspection), Technical Sublieutenant Uchida Isamu (hull), engineer Jōjima Seiichirō (fitting-out), engineer Miyagawa Hideto (chief of dock), engineer ōtsu Yoshinori (hull), assistant engineer Nakata Taizō (design)

Fourth row, from left: Technical Sublieutenant Kawada Takeshi (hull), Technical Sublieutenant Okabe Toshimasa (fitting-out), Technical Sublieutenant Minami Kazue (fitting-out), Technical Sublieutenant Hamano Kazuo (fitting-out), engineer Tani Michihiro (design), director Satō (clerical work, civilian).

Technical Sublieutenant Fukui Shizuo is standing in the third row, wearing working clothes, and is marked with a cross. He belonged to the staff of Lieutenant Commander Saitō Kanjirō, and his publications are a basic source for all students interested in the IJN.

Photo taken shortly before launching on June 1, 1939. It shows the forward part of no. 2 slipway, with the forward poppet on the starboard side of the hull. Note the many tricing lines coming down from the deck and fixed to the poppet. The clocklike disk on the right side is a slip indicator and shows the slip of the cradle (as the combination of sliding ways, poppet, and blocks is called) to the ground ways (the fixed part constructed of heavy timbers over the whole length of the hull). Between the ground ways and the sliding ways, a layer of grease was applied to reduce the friction generated by the sliding down of the cradle on the ground ways. Note the width (depth) of the bilge keel and the nicely curved hull line.

Shōkaku just prior to launching on June 1, 1939. The decorative ball (*kusudama*) is still unbroken, and the name of the ship in *hiragana* is written on the hanging cloth. The ship was launched in the presence of the chief of the naval general staff, Prince Fushimi Hiroyasu; the navy minister, Admiral Yonai Mitsumasa; and the commander of the Yokosuka Naval District, Vice Admiral Hasegawa Kiyoshi. Note the imperial crest, a chrysanthemum, fitted on the bow. It was made of teak and painted using real gold, measuring 1,200 mm in diameter. *Sekai no Kansen*

Shōkaku slides down the slipway on June 1, 1939. The decorative kusudama has been broken, and seven doves and confetti of five different colors have been released. Note the rather large bulb. *Kure Maritime Museum*

When *Shōkaku* was about to be launched, she was suddenly hit by heavy rain with strong side winds that caused rather high waves coming in from the sea. Despite this, the ship was successfully launched at 14:30. Her launching weight was 18,315 metric tons, about 1,500 more than the battleship *Mutsu*, launched eighteen years earlier. *Sekai no Kansen*

Zuikaku is being launched at Kawasaki Heavy Industries Warship Works (*Jūkōgyō Kansen Kōjō*), Kōbe, on November 27, 1939. On September 14, 1939, Prince Takamatsu Nobuhito, unannounced, visited the shipyard and said that the naval general staff had decided that the construction period of *Zuikaku* should be shortened by six months, in order to complete her at the same time as *Shōkaku*. In response to this, it was decided to shorten the period by three months, which eventually made it possible to include her in the Pearl Harbor attack. *The Maru Special*

Shōkaku slides into the water in heavy rain. Work on the launching had started at 00:00, and the workers proceeded very carefully since *Shōkaku* was a very long ship. Until the time of launching, the temperature was sweltering, and it was sometimes sunny, and when the weather deteriorated it was decided to launch the ship early. *Kure Maritime Museum*

Shōkaku in the water after being launched. Since the launch had been rather violent because of the wind, it was decided to send down divers to inspect the hull. Luckily the hull was undamaged and work could proceed. *Shōkaku's* fitting-out officer was Captain Jōjima Takatsugu. *Kure Maritime Museum*

CHAPTER 5

General Arrangement

The general arrangement is sufficiently explained by the figures. Space restrictions do not permit us to deal with the characteristic features in detail, but some of them are outlined in the sections below.

Table 2: Principal Dimensions		
Length (m)		238.00 pp, 250.00 wl, 257.50 oa
Beam (m)		29.00 wl
Depth (m)		23.00
Flight deck	Length (m)	242.20
	Width (m)	29.00 amid, 18.00 fwd, 26.00 aft
Height above wl	Trial condition (m)	14.13
	Full load (m)	13.68
Hangars	Upper (m)	200 × 24 max
	Lower (m)	180 × 20 max
Displacement	Trial (tonnes)	29,800
	Full load (tonnes)	32,105
	Light load (tonnes)	24,170
	Suppl. light load (tonnes)	24,770
Draught (m)		8.87 (mean) trials, 9.32 full load
Freeboard	Forward (m)	10.00 (anchor deck)
	Amidships (m)	8.80 (upper hangar deck)
	Aft (m)	6.60 (boat deck)

Notes: pp = perpendiculars; wl = waterline; oa = over all; amid = amidships; fwd = forward; Suppl = Supplementary

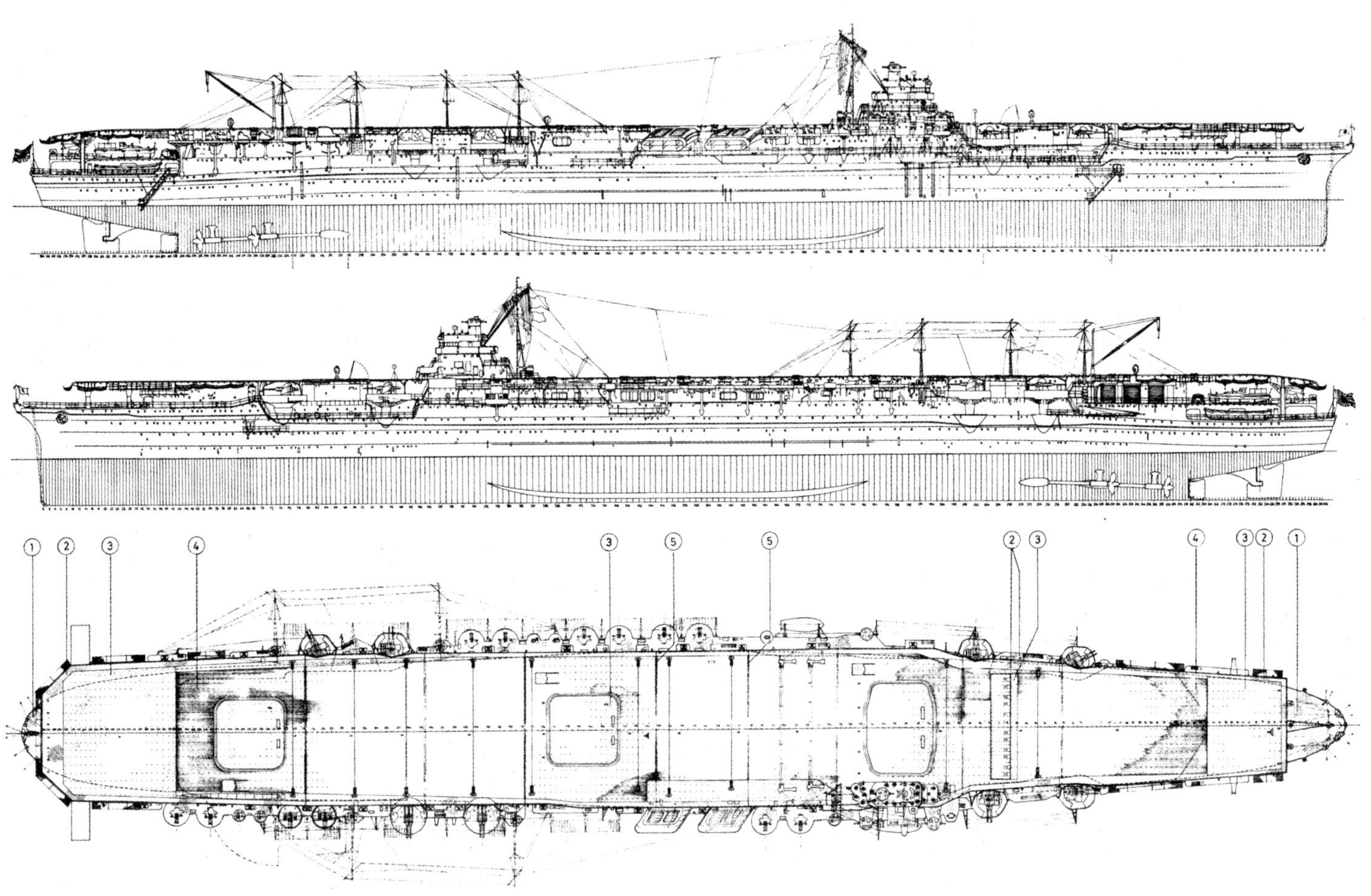

Side views and plan view of *Shōkaku* as built. *Michael Wünschmann*

Key: 1 = steel with nonskid paint on weather deck; 2 = steel with nonskid paint on galleries / deck edges; 3 = steel nonskid surface on flight deck / elevators; 4 = deck planking on flight deck; 5 = expansion joints in flight deck

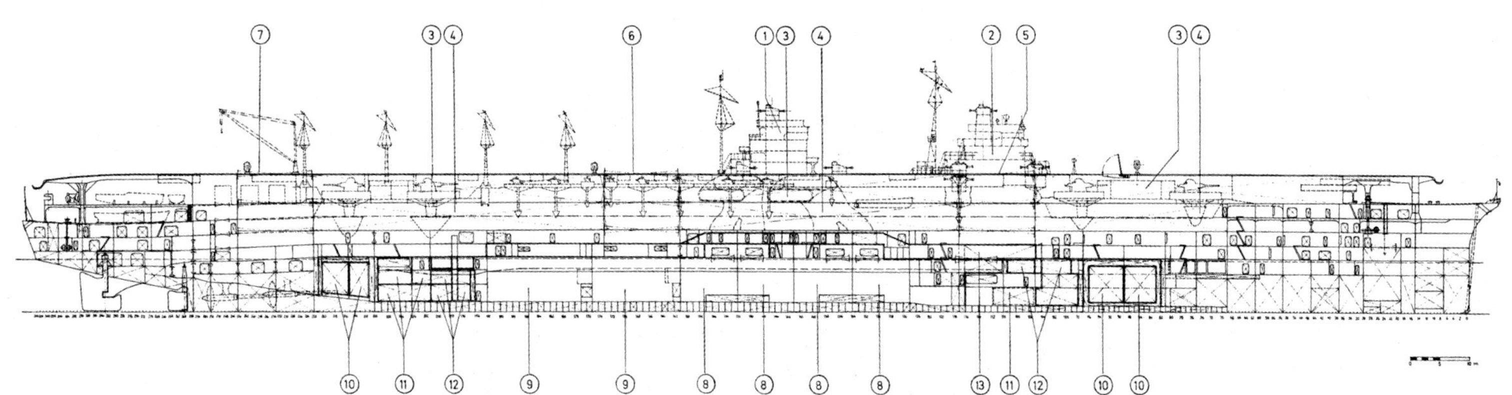

Inboard profile of *Shōkaku*. *Michael Wünschmann*

Key: 1 = position of island as designed; 2 = position of island as completed; 3 = upper hangar; 4 = lower hangar; 5 = forward aircraft elevator; 6 = center aircraft elevator; 7 = aft aircraft elevator; 8 = boiler rooms; 9 = engine rooms; 10 = avgas tank groups; 11 = air weapons magazines; 12 = magazines for antiaircraft ordnance; 13 = torpedo adjustment room

A very good view of *Shōkaku* anchored in Yokosuka Naval Port on August 23, 1941, two weeks after the commissioning ceremony, held on August 8. Pay attention to the shielded high-angle guns and machine guns aft of the two funnels—a precaution taken to protect the crew from smoke and hot gases. The canvas-covered guns forward of the funnels do not have such shields. Note also the removable funnel covers. The completion date was shortened by about three months in order to prepare her for war, and it is said that no delay was permitted even though the main engines and boilers were delivered late. Because some express work must have been necessary to complete her on schedule, this is probably the cause of her long stay in Yokosuka Naval Port. She is about to embark the commander in chief of the 1st Air Fleet (*Dai 1 Kōkū Kantai*), Vice Admiral Nagumo Chūichi, and will proceed on her maiden voyage to Ariake Bay.

A port side view of *Zuikaku* at Kōbe on September 25, 1941. According to Fukui Shizuo, this photo was presented as a memorial to a limited number of individuals involved in her construction in Kawasaki Shipyard. The open anchor deck forward of the hangar, the thick support posts below the flight deck, and the forward edge of the flight deck, approximately 10 m from the bow, were characteristic features of Japanese aircraft carriers. *Zuikaku's* fitting-out officer was Captain Yokokawa Ichihei.

A starboard view of the newly completed *Zuikaku* probably taken in Bungo Channel in October–November 1941. Note the downward-curved afterpart of the flight deck, with red-and-white stripes, the boat deck aft below the flight deck, and the large posts supporting the flight deck's overhang. *Zuikaku*'s scheduled completion date had to be put forward because of the late delivery of the main engines, boilers, and part of the auxiliary machinery. The propulsion unit of this class was remarkable because it developed the highest power (160,000 shp) in the IJN. The signal mast abaft the island and the wireless masts appear to be very delicate structures but were in fact rigid.

Zuikaku near Bungo Channel, probably on October 20, 1941. At this time, the carrier-based aircraft were training hard, and it can be seen that seawater is being sprayed on the hot funnel gases. The photo was probably taken from the battleship *Mutsu*. *Kure Maritime Museum*

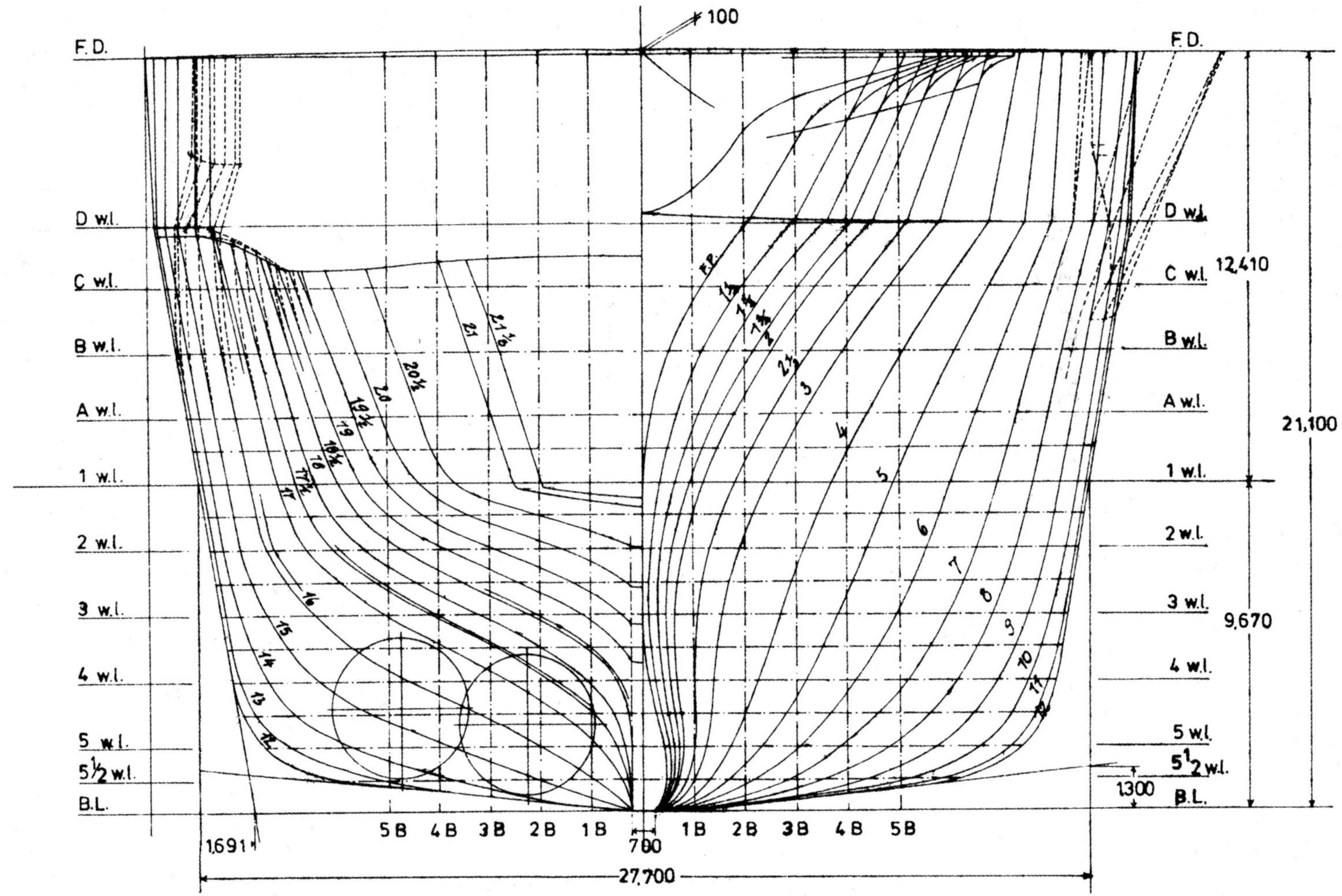

Lines. *Michael Wünschmann*

Flight Deck

The flight deck was 242.20 m long and 29 m wide, decreasing to 18 m at the bow and to 26 m aft; the flight deck area was roughly comparable to *Akagi* after conversion. The flight deck was fitted with wood planking except for forward of the first aircraft lift and abaft the after lift.[9] The afterpart of the steel deck had a nonskid paint that had the appearance of rough emery paper, and the fore part was covered with thin strips of steel 200 mm long and 16 mm wide, welded to the deck at various angles.

Like the British Royal Navy, the IJN favored enclosed hangars, in contrast to the open hangars of the later US Navy carriers. The upper hangar deck was generally the strength deck—the sole exceptions being *Taihō* and *Shinano*—and the flight deck was made as light as possible structurally. The criterion for flight deck strength was a landing load twice the weight of the heaviest type of aircraft in current service. This was achieved by placing transverse beams as supports at every frame and making every other beam a heavy one of about 460 mm depth. Longitudinals, crisscrossing the beams, provided additional strength for the transverse structure but had a relatively wide spacing. This light structure was an essential element in the conception of the sides of the upper hangar as "blowout walls."

The flight deck extended nearly the full length of the hull, and in order to withstand the hogging and sagging forces to which it was subjected when the ship rolled and pitched, it was divided into nine sections by fitting eight expansion joints from close to the bow to just abaft the after lift.

It was accepted that the higher the flight deck above the waterline, the better for the operation of aircraft. On the other hand, the greater the "sail" area when the ship was subjected to crosswinds, the greater the angle of heel.[10] It was decided that the height of the flight deck above the waterline should be at least 12 m, and preferably 13 m. In the final design the height in trial condition was 14.13 m, reducing to 13.68 m in the full-load condition due to the increased draft.[11]

The anchor deck (the forward part of the upper hangar deck, which extended below the flight deck to the bow) was kept clear of fittings that might obstruct takeoff; a theoretical line with an angle of 13° was drawn from the forward edge of the flight deck to the top of the bow, and no fitting was allowed to project above the line. This requirement originated from experience with *Akagi* in her original three-level flight deck configuration; when planes took off from the upper flight deck, they occasionally struck the foremost part of the lower flight deck on takeoff. However, the arrangement of the flight deck of the Shōkaku class was radically different, and there was only a very short distance between the forward edge of the flight deck and the bow, so the comparatively small angle of 13° was sufficient.

It was intended to fit two catapults, and the necessary preparatory work recesses, covers, guides, etc. were carried out. The IJN began studies of what was called "warship takeoff forward equipment" (*kanpatsu sokushin sōchi*) when *Kaga* was built, but failed to develop an operational catapult before the end of the war. The difficulty of installing catapults over the expansion joints is often given as a reason, but this may be only part of the truth.

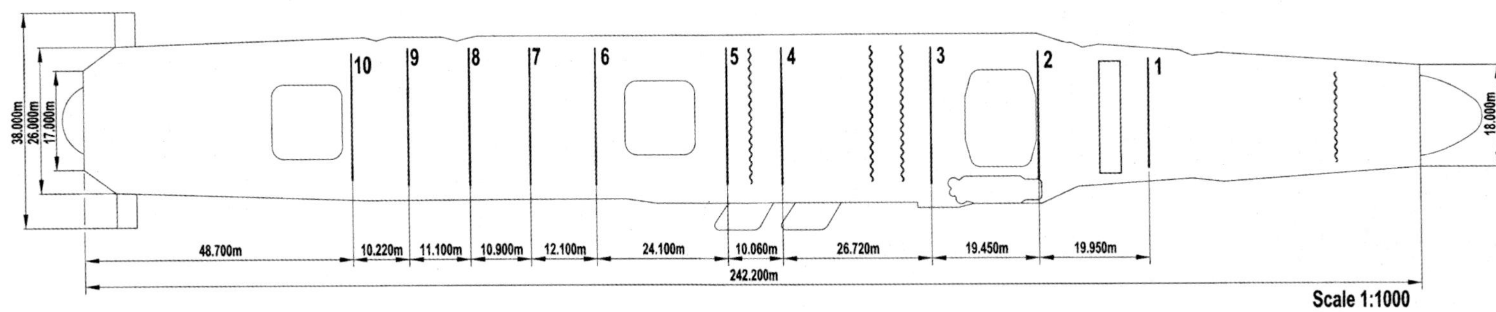

The flight deck of the Shōkaku class. Size: 242.20 × 29.00 m; aircraft elevators: 3 (forward, 13 × 16 m; middle, 13 × 12 m; aft, 13 × 12 m); hangars: 2 (upper and lower); aircraft capacity: 18 fighters, 27 dive-bombers, 27 torpedo bombers; arrester gear: Kure-type model 4 (10 engines, 10 cables); crash barriers: 5 *Kūshō* -type model 3 (3 fixed, 2 movable); windbreaks: 1; bomb hoists: 2 lift type

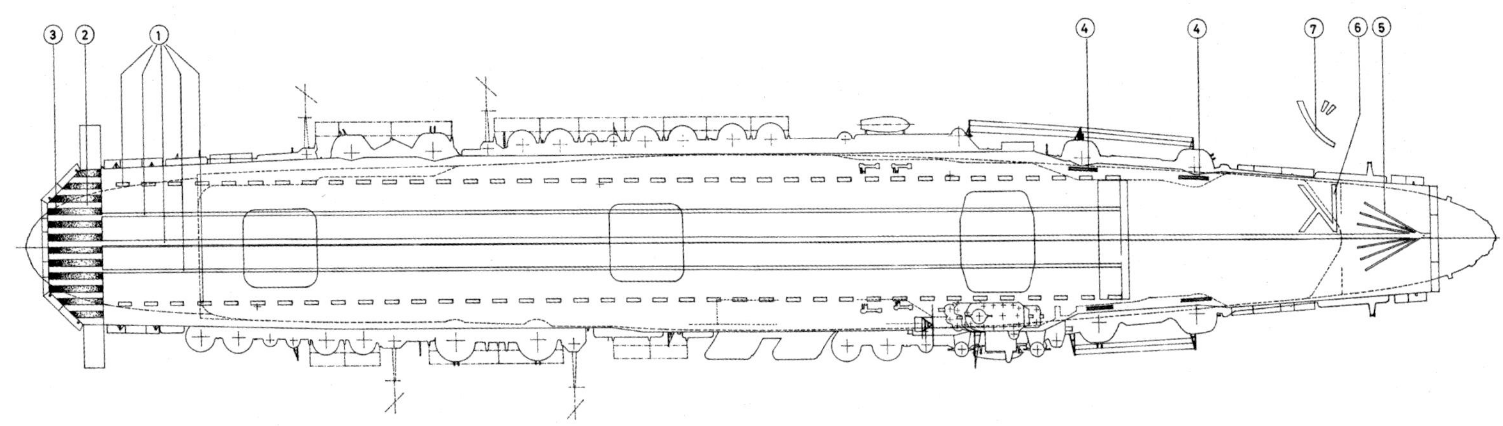

Flight deck markings. *Michael Wünschmann*
Key: 1 = marking lines; 2 = white lines; 3 = red lines; 4 = high-angle gun markings (red and white); 5 = wind direction indicator (white); 6 = *Zuikaku*; 7 = *Shōkaku*

Zuikaku is about to leave Hitokappu Bay on November 26, 1941, and the crew is about to take up one of the huge 10.7-ton bower anchors. Two of the flight deck main supports are visible, and to the right is a fleet oiler. The sailors are apparently feeling the effects of the bitter-cold weather. The departure was delayed by an hour because a rope was caught up in a propeller. *The Maru Special*

Aircraft Elevators

Three elevators were fitted: forward, center, and aft. The forward lift measured 13 m (L) × 16 m (W), and the center and after lifts 13 m (L) × 12 m (W). The forward lift was larger so that aircraft landing could be struck down quickly with their wings still deployed. The lifts were operated by electric motors, and speed was controlled by a Ward-Leonard system. The platform was counterweighted, and the two hoisting wires at each corner of the platform were connected to winches mounted on the same shaft and driven by a motor located in the lift pit. With a maximum speed of 50 m/sec., the lift took fifteen seconds to be raised from the lower hangar deck to the flight deck. The lift platforms were secured to the flight deck by large brackets that were mounted on hinges and swung under the platform manually. Because of the rolling and pitching of the ship, rollers were used in the guide paths, and buffers were also mounted to compensate for these movements. However, the lifts could still jam if exposed to major shocks, as evidenced by the bomb damage sustained by *Shōkaku* in 1942.

Aircraft Hangars with "Expansion Holes"

The increase of the depth permitted the arrangement of two aircraft hangars, one above the other. The upper hangar was 4.85 m high, the lower 4.7 m, which was the maximum height used in Japanese aircraft carriers. Each was divided into three compartments by the forward and center lifts. The upper hangar was about 200 m long from the aft elevator to the anchor deck, and the width varied between 18.5 m (above the boiler rooms) and 24 m. The plans of *Shōkaku* show the decrease in width resulting from the redesign of the island. The lower hangar was shorter, with the length of the forward section being reduced by about 20 m to serve as crew quarters. The width of this hangar varied between 17.5 and 20 m. The total hangar floor area of 5,545 m^2 permitted the stowage of the required seventy-two (plus twelve reserve) aircraft, provided that the planned types were embarked. Blueprints prove the decrease of the width caused by the redesigning.

The IJN recognized the heavy damage a bomb hit would cause to the flight and hangar decks and also to the hangar walls. The protection of areas as large as the hangar walls was impossible because of top-weight considerations, so a means of releasing the expanding detonation gases was considered the only effective countermeasure. The basic idea was to make the supports for the flight deck (pillars) as strong as necessary, and the plates between them very thin so that they would be blown out in the event of an internal explosion, thus providing expansion openings for the gas pressure and minimizing damage. Prior to the completion of the Shōkaku class, Kure Navy Yard carried out experiments in August 1940, using large-scale models. The results may be summarized as follows:[12]

(1) The expansion of the detonation gases within the entire volume of the hangar means that a lower maximum pressure is attained. Many expansion openings should therefore be distributed over the whole area. The amount of pressure reduction cannot be accurately measured because no comparative experiments are undertaken under the same conditions, and a new experiment has to be carried out at each time. However, due to the rapid transformation of the explosive from solid into gas condition (within 1/10,000 of a second), a marked reduction in the intensity of the pressure wave cannot be expected unless the openings are very large.

(2) The proposal to reduce the extent of the damage by expansion openings is effective, provided the pressure can escape not only horizontally but also vertically.

(3) The larger the expansion openings per 100 m^3 volume, the better. However, it is estimated that 1.2 m^2 per 100 m^3 should be sufficient. The cover plates should therefore measure approximately 1.3 m × 0.8 m.

(4) During the experiments, the covers were blown out at 0.75 kg/cm^2 pressure. Pressures below this figure will not be generated by an explosion; the normal pressure will be about 3 kg/cm^2.

On the basis of these conclusions, the upper hangar walls of the Shōkaku class (and later also *Taihō*) had so-called expansion openings. However, *Shōkaku*'s bomb damage at the Battle of the Coral Sea (May 1942) and the later Battle of Santa Cruz (October 1942) demonstrated that even though the "blowout wall" idea worked, in both cases the flight deck was destroyed, mainly because the assumption that a bomb would pierce the lightly structured flight deck and detonate only when it struck the upper hangar (strength) deck was in error. Moreover, points 1 and 2 in the above conclusions suggest that the IJN did not expect too much from the blowout plate system.

Island Bridge

According to Fukuda's statement at the aforementioned technical conference that "the structure of the bridge is the same as *Hiryū* in the final study, which involved a full-scale-sized model," the bridge closely resembled that of *Hiryū*. For a ship the size of the Shōkaku class, the floor area of the four decks was barely adequate, and the briefing of the air crews, which should have taken place in the air operations room on the second deck, had to be moved to the flight deck prior to major strikes.

The aft end of the island was 166 m from the aft edge of the flight deck, and the island projected 2.7 m onto the flight deck, so the distance between the island and the centerline was only 11.3 m, and the overall width of the flight deck was reduced to 26.2 m at this point. These figures provide further evidence that the island had to be relocated 1 m inboard because of the redesign.

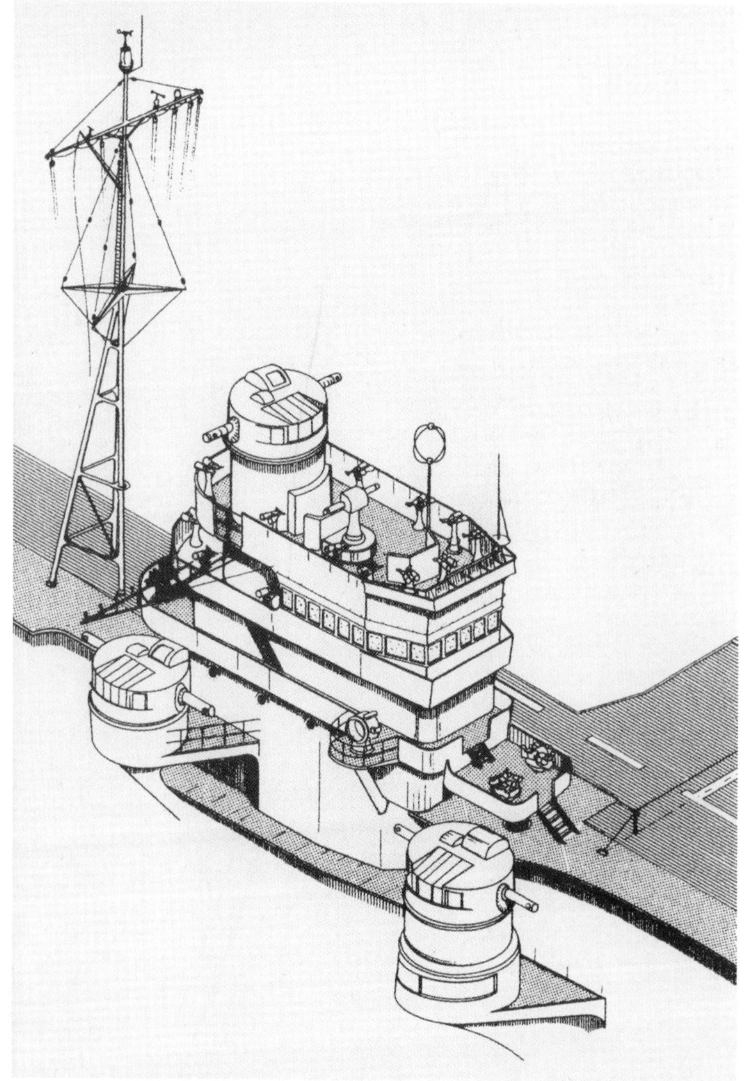

Bridge structure and signal mast of *Shōkaku*. Note the three type 94 high-angle fire control systems at the sides of the flight deck and on top of the open bridge. The latter was relocated to the opposite side of the flight deck and replaced by the mattress antenna for the type 21 radar. *Wilhelm Besch*

Profile and plan (at flight deck level) of bridge structure.
Hasegawa Tōichi
Key: 1 = D/F loop antenna; 2 = radio antenna; 3 = wind baffle; 4 = air defense command station deck; 5 = working light; 6 = compass bridge deck; 7 = lower bridge deck; 8 = flight deck; 9 = 2 kW signal light; 10 = loudspeaker; 11 = blackboard; 12 = supports; 13 = operation and sea chart room; 14 = meteorological operation room; 15 = storeroom for hand flags; 16 = signal light; 17 = type 94 high-angle fire control system; 18 = flashing signal light

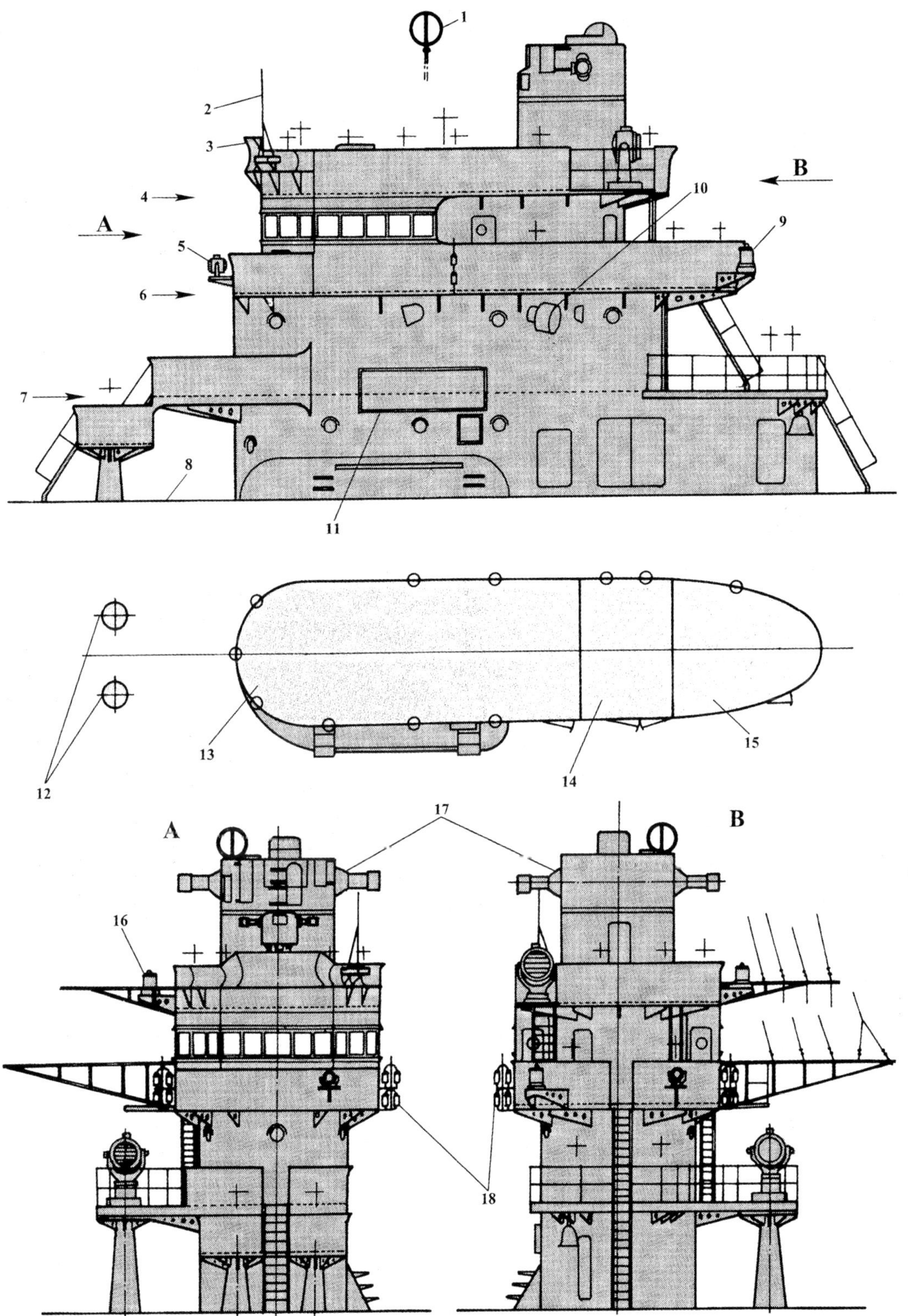

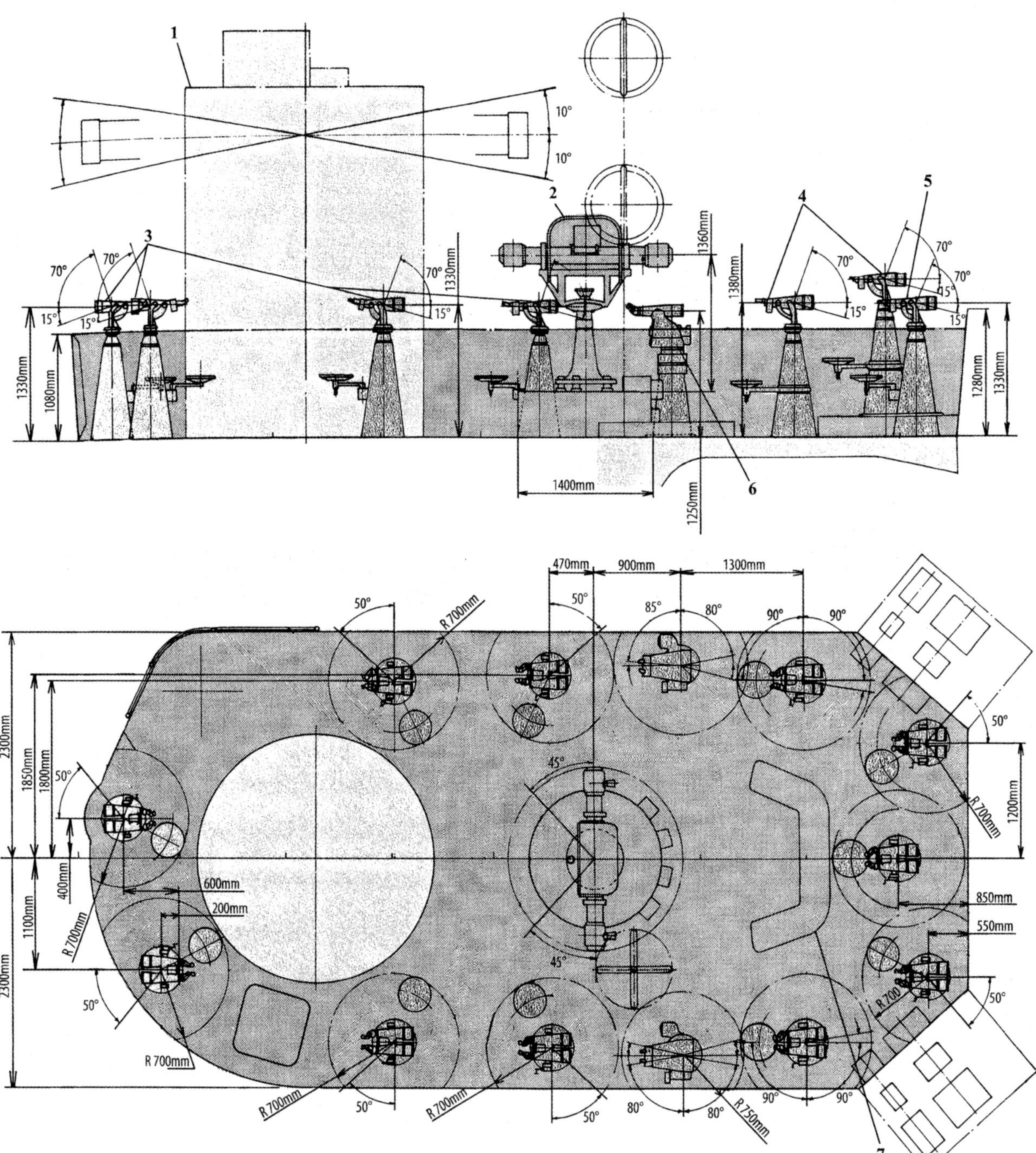

Air defense command station on *Shōkaku. Hasegawa Tōichi*
Key: 1 = type 94 high-angle fire control system; 2 = type 96 1.5 m rangefinder; 3 = 12 cm high-angle binoculars (later replaced by 12 cm high-angle binoculars, model 5); 4 = 12 cm binoculars (later replaced by 12 cm high-angle binoculars, model 13); 5 = 12 cm high-angle binoculars (later replaced by 12 cm high-angle binoculars, model 5); 6 = 12 cm high-angle binoculars for high-angle guns commandant; 7 = screen for mounting of receivers and transmitters

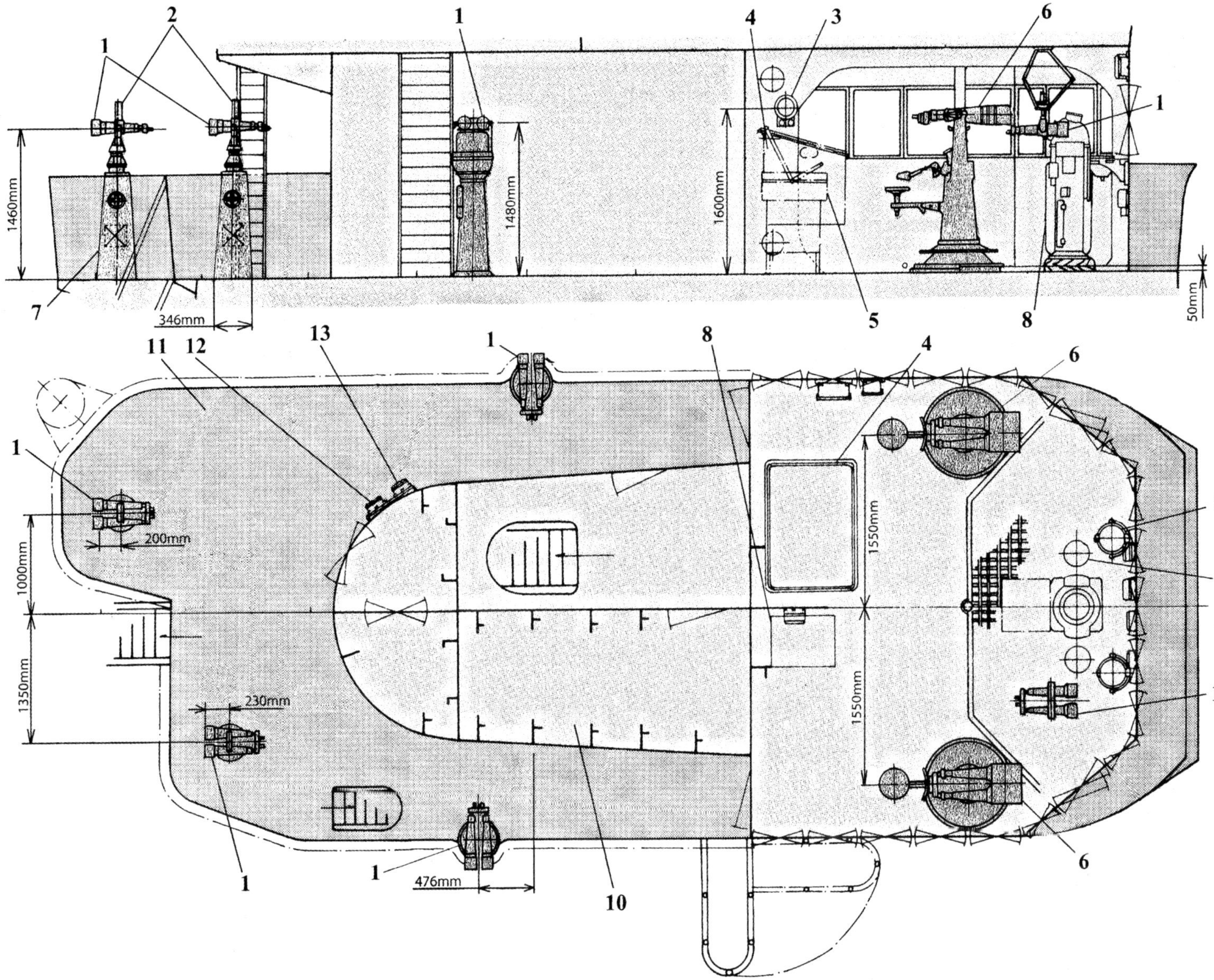

Compass bridge on *Shōkaku. Hasegawa Tōichi*
Key: 1 = 12 cm binoculars; 2 = type 97 Yamakawa light, model 1; 3 = type 92, no. 2 rangefinder with no. 1 range receiver; 4 = sea chart table; 5 = war diary table; 6 = 18 cm binoculars, model 13; 7 = type 97 Yamakawa light; 8 = type 93, no. 3 magnetic compass; 9 = gyro compass, model 5, modification 1; 10 = command station; 11 = control station for takeoff and landing; 12 = wind direction receiver; wind speed receiver

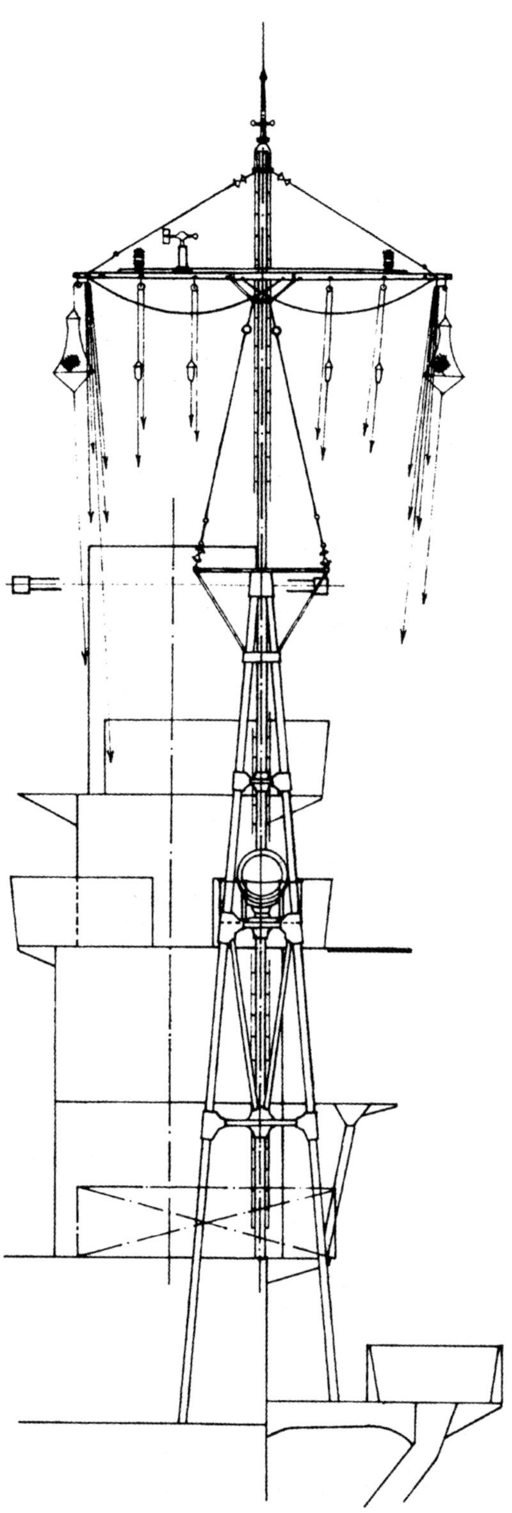

The tripod signal mast abaft the island structure. On top is a thin lightning conductor, and immediately below it, the wind strength (speed) indicator. In the thick part below it and above the yardarm is the connecting box for transmitting wind strength and wind direction to the receiving box in the island structure. On top of the yardarm are two 2 kW daylight signaling lamps and the wind direction indicator. The two rather large objects hanging from the yardarm are speed cones (*sokuryokuhyō*), used to indicate engine speed to ships astern (the higher the faster). The 60 cm signal light was unique for *Zuikaku*. *Michael Wünschmann*

Hoisted signal flags on the signal mast aboard a Shōkaku-class carrier. *Gakken*

Zuikaku in Hitokappu Bay off the Kuriles on November 22, 1941. Both *Shōkaku* and *Zuikaku* were assembled here prior to the Pearl Harbor attack. Ropes are stretched around the wall of the island as part of battle preparations. A direction-finding (D/F) loop antenna can be seen on the flight deck, and another loop antenna is fitted on the bridge structure. The thin antenna on the bridge structure is a radio mast. The object on the flight deck covered with white canvas is a floodlight *(shōmeitō)*.

A type 0 ("Zero"/"Zeke") A6M3 model 32 fighter is taking off from *Shōkaku* during the Battle of Santa Cruz in October 1942. Note the checker plates at the edge of the flight deck. The island bridge structure is comparatively small. Atop the bridge structure, a type 94 high-angle gun fire control system is mounted. To control the eight type 89 40 cal., 12.7 cm high-angle guns, *Shōkaku* had a total of four such fire control systems. This photo was official, and it was released by the IJN. *Sekai no Kansen*

Zuikaku as flagship of the 5th Carrier Division—note the rear admiral's flag. It is not certain when this photo was taken, but it is presumed that it is from the Battle of the Coral Sea or earlier, judging from the dress of the sailors. The signal mast abaft the island structure has a platform with a 60 cm signal light, and this was a distinguishing feature of *Zuikaku* since *Shōkaku* did not have such a platform. *The Maru Special*

Zuikaku at Kure on July 14, 1942. The crew has gathered on the flight deck to show their appreciation of the commander of the 5th Carrier Division, Rear Admiral Hara Chūichi. He has announced his resignation as commander of the division. The 5th Carrier Division was disbanded after the disastrous Battle of Midway, and the ships were assigned to the 3rd Fleet (*Dai 3 Kantai*), 1st Carrier Division (*Dai 1 Kōkū Sentai*), commanded by Vice Admiral Nagumo Chūichi.

The crew of *Zuikaku* is waving farewell to Rear Admiral Hara Chūichi on July 14, 1942. The type 94 fire control system is painted white, a practice that was discontinued in the summer of 1943. The crews' dress is typical for carrier operations in the South Pacific.

This photo of *Shōkaku* was taken on Navy Day, May 27, 1943, and shows the huge mattress antenna of the type 21 radar on top of the bridge structure. As result, the type 94 high-angle gun fire control system previously mounted there was relocated to the port side of the flight deck. Another type 21 radar mattress was placed in a recess in the flight deck, at a position previously occupied by a type 96 110 cm searchlight. The mattress could be lowered or raised just like the searchlight. The fitting of retractable searchlights and radar antennas was a feature of the IJN's aircraft carriers. According to Fukui Shizuo, the assembled sailors wear the formal uniform, and the large ensign on the signal mast indicates that they are celebrating the Battle of Tsushima. Note that there is no 60 cm signal light fitted on the signal mast.

The commander in chief of the Combined Fleet (*Rengō Kantai*), Admiral Koga Mineichi, is talking with the commander of the 3rd Fleet, Vice Admiral Ozawa Jisaburō (*back to camera*), on the afterpart of the compass bridge on *Zuikaku* in August–October 1943. The instrument shown is a wind direction and wind force (speed) receiver box.

Boat Storage

Boat stowage was a particular problem for a carrier. Because of the characteristic shape of the hull, twelve boats were stowed on the stern. These were as follows:

- three 12 m motor boats (*naikatei*)
- three 12 m motor launches (*naikaranchi*)
- one 8 m motor launch
- one 6 m service boat (*tsūsen*)
- two 9 m whalers
- two 13 m special transport boats (*tokusen unkatei*)

The boats were handled by 4-metric-ton cranes of the folding type and four boat hoists; there were also two 2.5-metric-ton motor winches and a single 1-metric-ton motor winch.

CHAPTER 6

Protection

The horizontal and vertical protection of the vital part and the underwater protection was roughly comparable to contemporaneous heavy cruisers (CAs), and much superior to the past aircraft carriers. The horizontal protection was formed by an armored deck that extended from the forward to the aft aviation gasoline tank groups, and thus it also covered the machinery spaces and bomb, torpedo, and ammunition magazines. Upon a base of 25 mm Ducol steel (DS), an armored deck of New Vickers noncemented (NVNC) and copper-alloy noncemented (CNC) plating was placed on two levels: at lower deck level above the machinery spaces, as far as the forward aircraft lift, and at the level of the platform deck forward and aft, above the magazines. The thickness varied from 105 mm (above the avgas tanks) to 132 mm (above the magazines). Above the machinery spaces, CNC armor of 65 mm thickness and tapered toward the sides was used. As belt armor, 46 mm CNC formed the outer hull plating over the area covered by the armored deck (lower deck). The magazines, which were outside this area, were protected by 165 mm thick NVNC armor with an inclination up to 25° and tapered from 75 to 55 mm. The lowermost part was connected to 50 mm DS. The side armor went down from the armored deck to the horizontally arranged bulkhead, of 8 mm thickness, which separated the watertight compartments (WTC) from the oiltight (OT) ones below the waterline. It was about 5 m high in this area; outside the height was reduced to about 3 m.

Underwater protection was provided by the multiple-plate (layered) method. The arrangement of air and liquid layers was the first such application in a Japanese warship and deserves special attention. Inboard of the outer hull plating there were four longitudinal bulkheads: inner bottom, wing passage bulkhead, protective (torpedo) bulkhead, and splinter bulkhead. According to Report S-01-9, "Underwater Protection" of the US Naval Technical Mission to Japan, p. 74, the protective bulkhead comprised two plates riveted together, the outer 18 mm and the inner 12 mm thick. This corresponds to the 30 mm DS stated in various Japanese sources, but the authoritative *Shōwa Zōsenshi*, vol. 1, p. 537, gives the thickness as "30–42 mm" without stating details. The protective bulkhead covered the entire depth from the armored deck to the outer hull plating. The thickness of the inner bottom, wing passage, and splinter bulkhead was 8 mm each. The spaces between the outer and inner bottom and between the protective bulkhead and the splinter bulkhead were divided into watertight compartments (WTCs); the spaces between the inner bottom, wing passage, and protective bulkhead were partitioned by transverse bulkheads and used as oil fuel tanks (OTs). The depth of the wing passage, which served as an expansion space for the detonation gases, was about 2.2 m. It was normally filled with oil fuel but was emptied in battle condition. The protective strength of this arrangement along the machinery spaces was calculated to have a joint efficiency of 53% against 450 kg of explosive. The weight of water that would flood these compartments in the event of a single torpedo hit was expected to be about 900 metric tons (the shaded area in the drawing). Damage to the protective bulkhead was expected, but flooding of the machinery spaces should have been prevented by the splinter bulkhead. This assumption was based on the results of model experiments[13] but was of doubtful validity; later experiments demonstrated that "the objective could not be attained completely" (*Shōwa Zōsenshi*). For more details, please refer to the enclosure.

Following the loss of *Taihō* and *Shōkaku* in the Battle for the Mariana Islands, unusual measures were taken to enhance the protection of the avgas tank groups forward and aft in *Zuikaku*. According to Fukui Shizuo, bulges of 600–800 mm depth were fitted below the waterline in the area of the tanks and filled with concrete. Hull resistance was significantly increased, and the bulges also caused a strange wave formation around the hull. However, high speed was no longer a key factor; survivability was the only factor that counted. Despite these measures, *Zuikaku* sank two months later, having sustained multiple torpedo and bomb hits.

Damage Control System

Shōkaku and *Zuikaku* were the first carriers to have special compartments as part of the damage control system. The IJN began the installation of a damage control system from *Sōryū* onward—it was limited to the use of oil fuel tanks—but when the studies for the battleships of the Yamato class were undertaken, the system was greatly expanded. As with *Yamato*, the number and capacity of the heavy oil feed pumps were increased, with a view to moving oil between the tanks for trim control, and the pipe systems were improved to permit this operation. Separate compartments were used for the control of list. However, as shown in the drawing of the underwater protection system, the heavy oil tanks outboard of the machinery spaces were emptied under battle conditions, and in the event of a torpedo hit, undamaged tanks could be flooded correspondingly as a supporting measure.

Enclosure

Underwater protection arrangement of the Shōkaku class (single-plate method, straight type, joint efficiency 53%)[14]

To prevent the destruction of the protective (torpedo) bulkhead by multiple splinters generated by the breakup of the structure in the immediate vicinity of the detonation point and the direct impact of the detonation gases, systematic model experiments were carried out starting in 1935. Because the speed of splinters is substantially unaffected by the width of the air space, and because within the usual width of the air space (~3,000 mm) the force of the detonation has considerable destructive power, it was of the utmost importance to find protective methods to reduce the effect of the splinters before they struck the protective bulkhead. In addition, damage might be increased by the inrush of water through the hole caused by the detonation, thereby underlining the importance of an undamaged bulkhead.

In the end, the IJN arrived at the following conclusions:

(1) A water layer is more effective than either an air layer or a bulge filled with watertight steel tubes.

(2) The depth of the water layer should be 600 mm, and the compartment should be filled to no more than 90% of the capacity. (Experiments with deeper layers and capacity filling brought about inferior results; also, the deeper the water layer, the narrower the air space, which was important for the expansion of the detonation gases and, hence, the dispersion of their force.)

(3) The water layer should be against the face of the protective bulkhead, with the void outboard of it. In this way, the water layer distributes the force of concussion over the entire surface of the protective bulkhead, thus greatly reducing the pressure per unit. In addition, the speed of splinters is reduced, and much of the heat of the gases is consumed. The larger the width of the outer air space, the greater the expansion of the detonation gases—as stated in "2."

(4) A straight bulkhead is superior to the curved type.

(5) It is very difficult for the protective bulkhead to resist the detonation pressure and maintain watertightness at the same time. To guarantee watertightness, an additional watertight holding bulkhead ("backplate," or *seita*) should be fitted inboard of the protective bulkhead.

(6) From the point of view of weight, it would be uneconomical to carry water in the "water layer," so heavy oil is used instead. As the fuel oil is consumed, it must be replaced by water in order to maintain the same level of protection—experiments had shown no combustion of fuel near the point of detonation.

It was concluded that the thickness of the protective bulkhead could be reduced by 50% if a liquid, as opposed to an air layer, was used. It was also calculated that flooding would be reduced by about 30%.

If the conclusions in the study above are compared with the system devised for the Shōkaku class, it is evident that the arrangement adopted for the carriers was broadly in line with the findings, but that the width of the air space was insufficient, while the depth of the water/oil layer was excessive. By reducing the depth of the liquid layer to 600 mm, the air space (i.e., the emptied oil tanks) could have been increased to 2,800–3,200 mm, and by increasing the thickness of the protective bulkhead from 30 to 42 mm, the designed resistance (against 450 kg explosive) would have been attained in accordance with the formula developed from the model experiments.

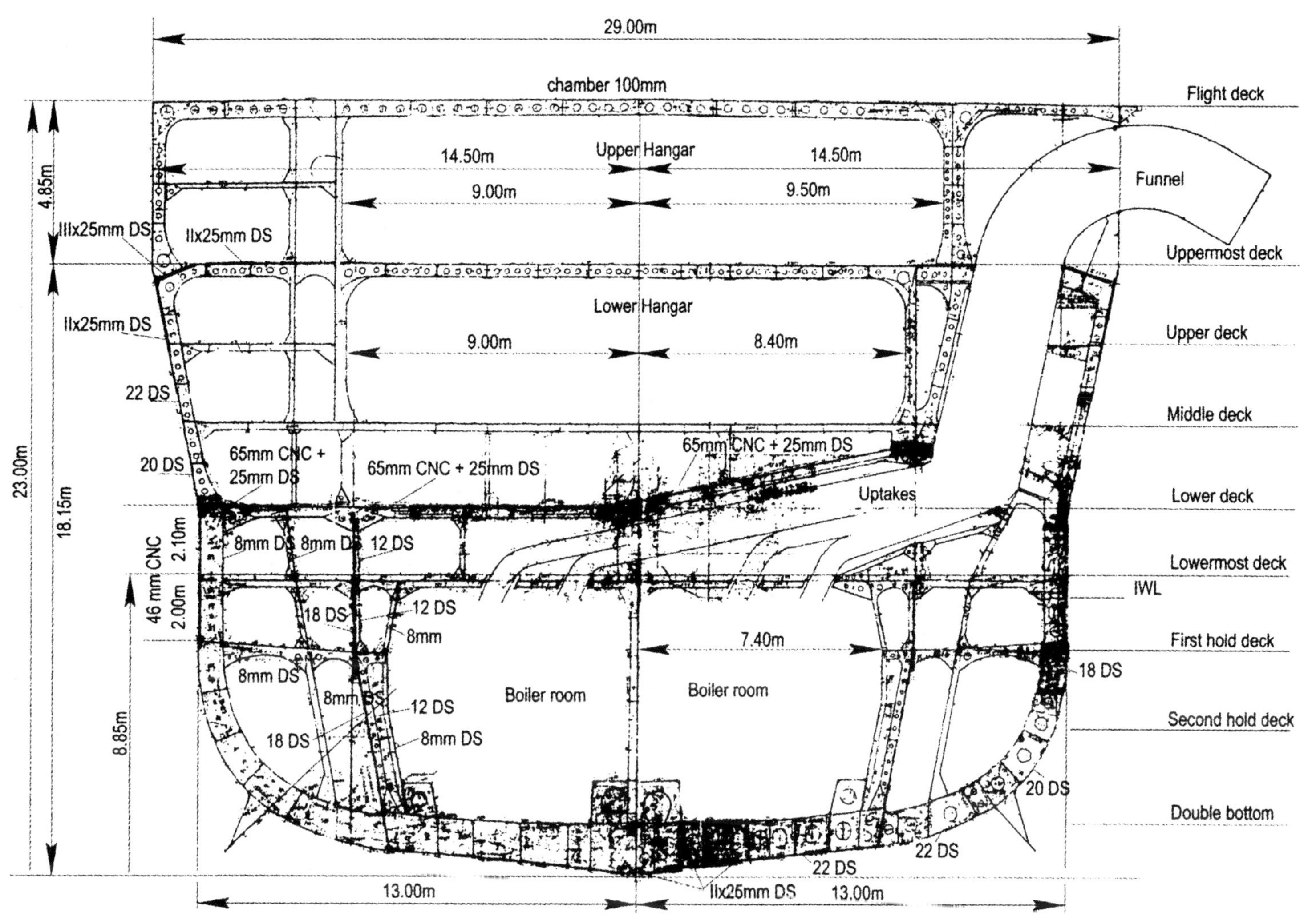

Midship section of *Shōkaku. Adapted from official plans*

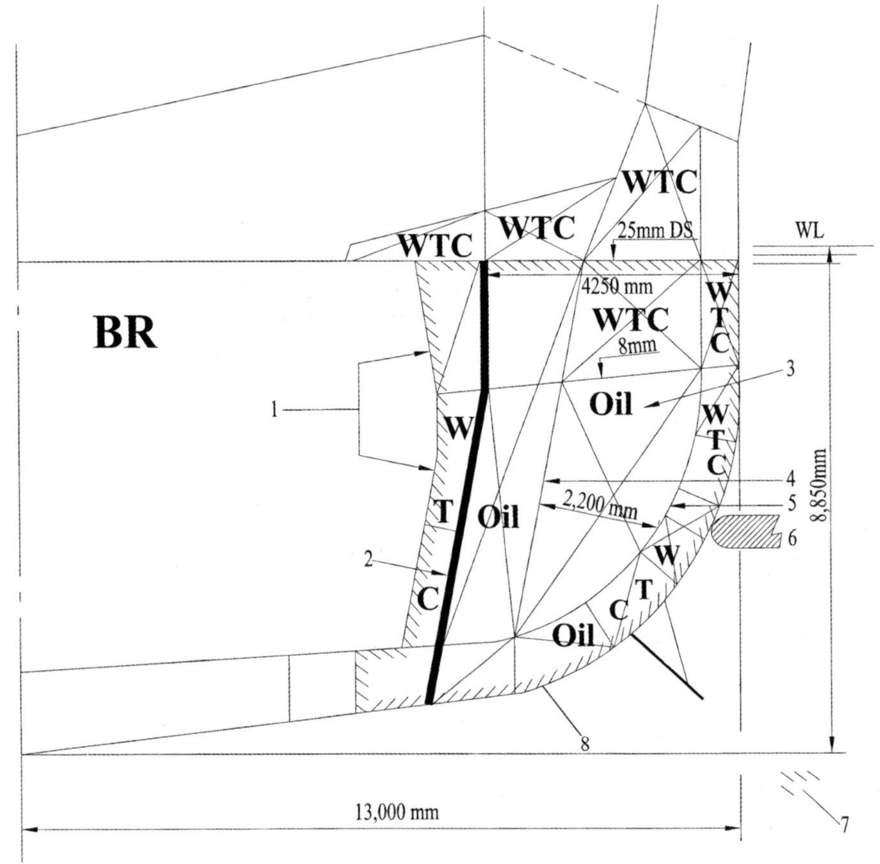

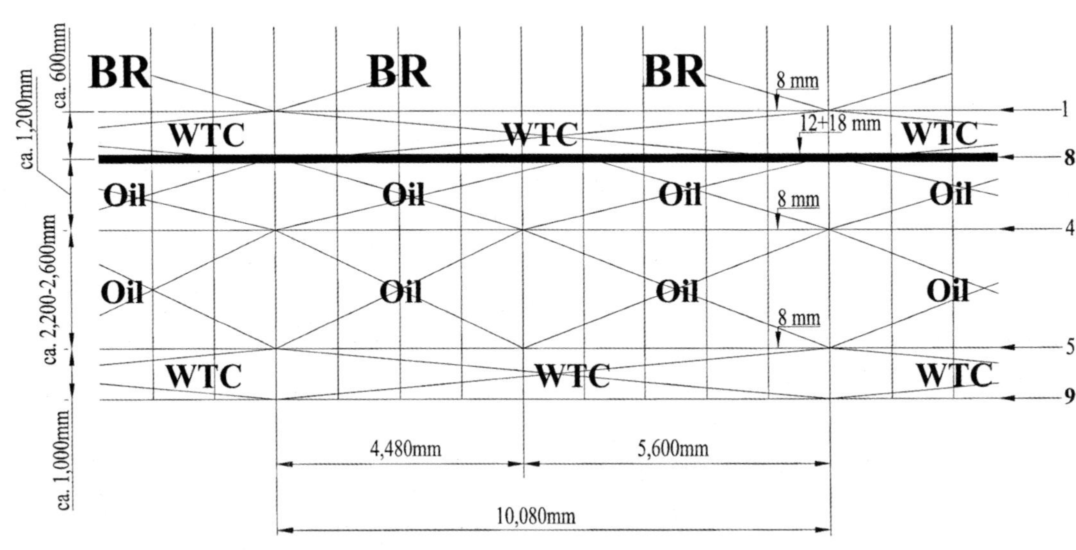

Underwater protection arrangement of the Shōkaku class. *Upper*, section at boiler room; *lower*, plan view. *Waldemar Trojca*
Key: 1 = backplate (holding bulkhead), 8 mm; 2 = protective longitudinal bulkhead (torpedo bulkhead), 18 mm outside + 12 mm inside, riveted together; 3 = oil tank emptied in battle condition to generate expansion space for detonating gases; 4 = fore plate, 8 mm; 5 = inner bottom, 8 mm; 6 = torpedo warhead; 7 = shaded area indicates flooding after torpedo hit (~900 tons of water, but held by 8 mm holding bulkhead); 8 = outer bottom; BR = boiler room; WTC = watertight compartment

A photo of *Zuikaku* during training off ōita in Beppu Bay, taken from an airplane just after takeoff, probably on September 21, 1944. This photo and the next are part of a film called "Torpedo-bombers attack!" (*Raigekitai Shutsudō*), produced by Tōhō and released on December 7, 1944. The old aircraft carrier *Hōshō* was also used for this film. A triple 25 mm machine gun platform can be seen just below the forward part of the flight deck. Note the strange wave formation around the hull, caused by the new bulges.

A photo taken shortly after the previous one, showing *Zuikaku* and the plane-guard ship astern. *Zuikaku* was docked at Kure (no. 4 dock) on July 14, 1944, and left the dock on August 2. As a result of the Battle of the Marianas, bulges were fitted below the waterline and filled with concrete. Her antiaircraft armament was also significantly increased, and the signal mast was modified. Note the camouflage scheme, which was probably applied in late July 1944. After the filming, *Zuikaku* entered Olta on September 22.

CHAPTER 7

Hangar and Flight Deck Equipment[15]

Landing Guide Lights

Pilot landings were assisted by sets of guide lights. The equipment was used by day and at night, the intensity of the light being regulated according to the conditions. It comprised a pair of red lamps (*shōmontō* = stationary shining door) and a group of four blue lamps (*shōseitō* = vertical movable shining star); the former moved in the horizontal plane, while the latter was fixed. The lights were mounted on outriggers on both sides of the flight deck aft. The pilot aligned his aircraft with the landing path, using the parallel light of these arrays; the general angle of landing was between 4° and 6°.

Equipment for Night Landings

Besides landing guide lights, there was a red landing-mark light called *kambi* (stern-marking light). White deck lights were arranged along the centerline and at the sides of the flight deck; the latter were fluorescent tubes some 20 cm long with reflectors. The pilot was informed about wind speed via a separate signal lamp. In addition, searchlights could also be used to guide aircraft in; however, these were used sparingly, since they increased the danger that the carrier would be discovered by enemy aircraft or submarines.

Arresting Gear and Crash Barriers

Arrester gear (*chakkan seido sōchi*) was developed in order to slow an aircraft on landing. The flight decks of *Shōkaku* and *Zuikaku* were fitted with ten arrester wires connected to brake machinery of the Kure type 4 modification 2 (*Kure shiki yon gata kai ni*). This gear was developed by the Electric Research Division (*Denki Jikkenbu*) of Kure Navy Yard from July 1933 onward. It was a modified version of the Kure type model 1 and was fitted from 1938 onward. The Kure type model 5 arrester gear was also trialed but was not used operationally, so model 4 (and its modifications) was the last type of arrester gear to see service with the IJN.

During landing operations, the wires were suspended at a minimum height of 160 mm by raising bars at the outer edges of the flight deck. Each wire was led down over guide pulleys to an arresting-gear compartment below the lower hangar deck, where the two ends were led to the sides of a winding drum, inside which was a squirrel-cage rotor made of high-resistance bronze. The drum and squirrel cage rotated around a six-pole stator energized with 120 A at 120 V; at the maximum setting the specific setting was selected according to the weight of the aircraft (all Kure-type arresting gear used the same principle).

When the tailhook of a landing plane caught the horizontal wire, the drum made 1.5 turns and actuated the electric brake. The aircraft ran against the resistance of the brakes until its kinetic energy was exhausted, whereupon it came to a halt. The maximum distance for stopping an aircraft was 40 m; retardation power was 2 g. Maximum brake retardation speed was 30 m/sec., and maximum aircraft weight 4,000 kg. It took twelve seconds to return the wire to its original position.

If a plane failed to catch any of the arrester wires with its arresting hook, it was stopped by a crash barrier (*kassō seishi sōchi*). Three fixed barriers of the Naval Air Technical Arsenal type model 3 modification 1 (*Kūshō shiki san gata kai ichi kassō seishi sōchi*) were mounted as shown in the drawing in chapter 5. According to Fukui Shizuo, two mobile barriers were on board, but these are not listed in the official ship's book. This gear was developed by Navy Technical Air Arsenal (*Kōkūgijutsushō*) and was a kind of hydraulic brake equipment. Each fixed barrier had three wires (lower, center, and upper) that were stretched between two posts mounted at the sides of the flight deck. These posts were raised to the correct height and were lowered pneumatically. The wires were attached to a separate pneumatic-hydraulic arresting unit installed at the port side of the upper hangar deck. If an aircraft engaged the wires, a system of pulleys caused a ram to be pushed into a hydraulic cylinder, thus forcing oil through a series of constrictions into an air-loaded accumulator. The shape of the constrictions and the increasing pressure of the air resulted in rapid retardation, with much less movement in comparison to the arresting gear. The maximum braking distance was 7 m, and the maximum brake force was 4 g (i.e., twice that of the arrester gear), so damage to the aircraft was unavoidable. Maximum brake speed was 5 m/sec., maximum aircraft weight was 4,000 kg, and the barrier could be raised or lowered in 2.5 seconds.

Windbreak

Forward of the first aircraft lift there was a windbreak. This was raised when aircraft were on the flight deck, and was lowered into a recess flush with the deck during flight operations. Holes were drilled into some 30% of the surface area of the shield, and it could be kept in the raised position with wind speeds up to of 50 m/sec. (180 km/hr.). When this value was exceeded, it was lowered into the recess; it could be raised again in thirty seconds against wind speeds up to 35 m/sec. (126 km/hr.).

Aviation Gasoline Filling Positions

There were a number of avgas refueling points on the flight deck. They were supplied by two main gasoline lines, one for type A high-octane fuel (for starting up and high bursts of speed), the other for type B lower-octane fuel (for cruising). Sufficient fixed type A refueling stations were provided to ensure that any position could be reached with a 25 m flexible hose. For type B fuel, twice as many filling stations were provided. Hoses were fitted with pistol-type filling valves.

Firefighting Equipment

Fire was a particular hazard on board an aircraft carrier. Carriers had large amounts of aviation fuel stored not only in tanks (see "Protection") but sometimes even in drums in the hangar, so safety was a critical factor. Precautions taken ranged from the adoption of special casings for motors to avoid sparks that could ignite avgas fumes, to the separation of the hangars into several firefighting zones by fire curtains, the use of two different agents for firefighting (CO_2 and foam), and protection of avgas pipes and hoses. It should, however, be mentioned that the CO_2 system was largely useless, and fire was the main cause of the loss of the four aircraft carriers *Akagi, Kaga, Sōryū,* and *Hiryū* at Midway in June 1942. In the autumn of 1942 the Yokosuka Navy Yard started experiments with a foam system, inspired by the system aboard the German liner *Scharnhorst* (later rebuilt into the Japanese auxiliary aircraft carrier *Shinyō*). By this system, a "foam blanket" sprayed horizontally over aircraft proved much more effective. After improvements made by the Chemical Research Institute of the Navy Technical Research Institute, and following more experiments, the foam system was decided on in early November 1942, and when *Shōkaku* was repaired after the carrier battles in the autumn of 1942, it became the first carrier fitted with this system.[16]

Zuikaku leaving Hitokappu Bay bound for Hawaii on November 26, 1941. "Zero" fighters are lined up and their engines are covered. Note the planked deck with numerous tie-down points for aircraft, the white lines, and the aircraft elevator platform. *Shōkaku* is to the left. *The Maru Special*

"Zero" fighters are prepared to take off from *Zuikaku* on January 20, 1942, for the attack on Rabaul. *Zuikaku* and *Shōkaku* had left Truk on January 16 for Operation "R" (Rabaul). When off Kavieng on January 20, *Zuikaku* launched six fighters and nineteen D3A1 ("Val") dive-bombers to attack Rabaul and afterward headed for eastern New Guinea. *The Maru Special*

A view of *Zuikaku's* flight deck early on January 20, 1942, as she was heading for the launching point for the attack on Rabaul. Six "Val" dive-bombers are lined up on the flight deck's parking and engine warm-up area. Note the lowered radio masts and the two crash barriers lying flat on the deck. To the left, at the aft end of the lower bridge deck, are stored signal flags. *Shōkaku* can be seen just beyond the parked planes. *The Maru Special*

A "Zero" fighter aboard *Zuikaku* is about to take off during the Battle of the Coral Sea on May 8, 1942. When the *hikōchō* (air officer) on the bridge waved his white flag in the direction of the bow, the *shō-hikōchō* (deck launching officer) on the deck blew a whistle and then waved his red-and-white flags, ordering the aircraft handlers to remove the wheel chocks. The pilot then shouted, "*Ikimasu!*" ("I'm going!"), the chocks were removed, and the handlers ran to the deck-side shelters. The planes were then launched.

The "Zero" fighter of Lieutenant Commander Shingō Hideki, flight group leader, takes off from *Shōkaku* during the Battle of Santa Cruz on October 26, 1942. The single white line around the fuselage indicates that this plane belongs to *Shōkaku; Zuikaku*'s planes had two white lines. Note the folded-down crash barriers under the plane, and the expansion joint in front of the plane. Shingō participated in many battles, and after the war he served in the Japan Self-Defense Forces.

A B5N2 ("Kate") torpedo bomber takes off from *Zuikaku*. It is probably a photo taken during the Lae and Salamaua (eastern New Guinea) operations on January 21, 1942. After having completed these operations, *Zuikaku* and *Shōkaku* proceeded to cover the landings at Rabaul and Kavieng. *The Maru Special*

A type 99 dive-bomber ("Val") takes off from *Zuikaku* to attack Colombo on April 5, 1942. Note the flight deck markings and her distinctive identification mark on the left (ス). There is not much wind, and the sea is calm. The steam vent, indicating the wind direction, on the centerline forward is emitting steam.

On February 28, 1943, *Shōkaku* left the drydock at Yokosuka after having been repaired and refitted. On March 18, Lieutenant Commander Horiuchi Yasuo took a number of photos of *Shōkaku* during exercises in the Uraga Channel. In this photo the carrier is beginning to take a straight course, and the plane-guard destroyer is following astern. The plane-guard ship was to observe and rescue downed pilots—"dragonfly fishing" (*tonbo tsuri*). The starboard helm signal (a green ball) shows that the ship is not turning. *Kure Maritime Museum*

A photo by Lieutenant Commander Horiuchi Yasuo of *Shōkaku* during training on March 18, 1943, probably north of Uraga Channel, in the direction of Tokyo Bay. A type 97 torpedo bomber (*kankō*) is about to land. *Kure Maritime Museum*

A type 97 torpedo bomber ("Kate") is about to land aboard *Zuikaku* during the Battle of Santa Cruz on October 26, 1942. Note the arrester wires stretched across the flight deck, and the plane's lowered landing hook. The handling crew in the pocket observes the plane and may also be following the plane, with downed flaps, visible in the background.

The torpedo bomber has landed on the *Shōkaku* close to the middle elevator, and the arrester wires can be seen. The plane handlers are prepared to take care of the plane. The following day, March 19, *Shōkaku* left for Tokuyama. *Kure Maritime Museum*

Zuikaku during training in the Seto Naikai after her last refit in late summer of 1944. A type 0 fighter (*Reisen*) belonging to the 653rd Fighter Squadron (*653 Kū*) appears to make a fly pass (*furai pasu*)—a pseudo-touchdown. This was made in order for the pilot to learn how to master the airplane. Behind the carrier is a plane-guard ship. *Gakken*

During a lull in the Battle of Santa Cruz, crew members are cleaning the afterpart of *Zuikaku's* flight deck. Japanese flight decks were usually planked with *beimatsu* wood, commonly translated as Douglas fir, and the planks were left in their natural wood finish until the summer of 1944, when camouflage paint were applied. *Shōkaku* is seen trailing behind *Zuikaku*.

CHAPTER 8

Machinery

In order to attain the required speed of 34.5 knots, the turbines were designed to develop 160,000 shp on four shafts.[17] This was the highest output of any existing Japanese warship; it exceeded that of the Yamato class by 10,000 shp and of the Mogami-class cruisers by 8,000 shp. A striking feature of the propulsion plant was that the cruise turbines were designed for a speed of 26 knots.[18] An abbreviated account of the official "Engine Planning and Specifications for No. 3 Warship" (nineteen pages, including drawings) is provided below: Index (1) General hull specifications (omitted), (2) Engine layout, (3) Main engines, (4) Condensers, (5) Shaft connections and propellers, (6) Boilers, (7) Uptakes and funnels, (8) Auxiliary machinery, (9) Repair facilities, (10) Estimated weight of engines, (11) Acceptance run (omitted).

For the data, see the accompanying tables.

2. When steaming full ahead, 160,000 shp in total to be generated by four turbines and eight oil-burning boilers; boiler steam pressure to be 30 kg/cm^2 at 350°C. Length of the machinery spaces to be 74.22 m (engine rooms, 33.90 m; boiler rooms, 40.32 m—see drawing for details).

3. Main engines to have a four-shaft arrangement, with Kampon high-pressure (HP), intermediate-pressure (IP), and low-pressure (LP) turbines driving each shaft via reduction gearing. One set of turbines to be installed in each of the four engine rooms: the turbines driving the inner shafts to be installed in the aft engine rooms, and those driving the wing shafts in the forward engine rooms. Each propeller shaft to be provided with one cruising turbine connected to each HP turbine gear through the cruising turbine reduction gear and a claw coupling. The astern turbines to be housed within the casings for the LP turbines.

The following table shows the outline. But some surplus areas should be given, so as to be able to bear excess loading of about 10% at the nozzles of the first stage of the high-pressure turbine (HPT).

Table 3: Power Rating and Propeller Rpm

	Power rating (shp)	Total output (shp)	Power rating
Ahead continuous rate	40,000	160,000	300
Cruise full rate	4,000	16,000	139
Cruise overload	5,500	22,000	155
Cruise allowable full power	12,500	50,000	204
Astern full	10,000	40,000	190

Note: shp = shaft horsepower; rpm = revolutions per minute.

Table 4: Planned Steam Pressure, Vacuum and Steam Consumption

	Steam pressure (kg/cm^2)	Steam temperature (°C)	Condenser (top) (mm Hg)	Steam consumption (kg/h/shp)
Ahead full	26	335	700	3.7
Cruise full	26	335	725	4.5
Astern full	21	330	645	9.0

Table 5: Turbine specifications

	HP	IP	LP	Astern	Cruise
Type	Kampon, impulse, single flow	As HP	Kampon, impulse, compound flow	As HP	As HP
Turbine rpm	2.821	2.821	2.774	1.567	7,900
Propeller rpm	300	300	300	190	204
No. of stages	1 bucket wheel with double row; 2 bucket wheels with single row	4 bucket wheels with single row	As IP	1 bucket wheel with three row	1 bucket wheel with double row; 4 bucket wheels with single row
Max. pitch circle diameter (mm)	1,100	1,270	1,420	1,250	550
Distance between centres of bearings (mm)	1,460	1,410	2,885	2,885	1,030
Pressure of steam chamber (kg/cm²)	27.00	6.60	1.26	22.00	27.00
Pressure at 1st stage (kg/cm²)	11.50	4.45	0.74	–	9.00
Exhaust pressure (kg/cm²)	6.85	1.34	0.10	0.18	1.97

Notes

1. The type of the turbines is not stated in the original document but have been added for better understanding.
2. The rotation of the cruising turbines corresponds to the cruising allowable full power and the steam pressure to the cruising overload power.
3. The turbine blades were made of non-corrosive B (*otsu*) steel.
4. HP = High-pressure; IP = Intermediate-pressure; LP = Low-pressure.

Table 6: Specifications for reduction gearing

	Main reduction gearing			Cruise reduction gearing	
	Main gear wheel	HP + IP pinion	LP pinion	Main gear wheel	Pinion
Rpm	300	2,821	2,474	1,456	6,000
Pitch circle diameter of teeth (in)	114.8338	12.2118	13.9257	23.7553	5.7739
No. of teeth	536	57	65	144	35
Length of teeth (mm)		1,240		640	
Diametrical pitch (DP)		5.3887		7.00	
Helical angle (°)		29°58'51"		30°0'21.8"	
Reduction rate	1	9.404	8.246	4.114	

Note

Because the IJN lagged far behind in the manufacture of reduction gearing, Kure Navy Yard and Kawasaki, Kōbe, each purchased one large and one small gear-cutting machine (gear hobbler) (for wheels and pinions, respectively) from the German Reineker Co. to manufacture the gearing for the Shōkaku and Yamato classes. Precision testers for checking the teeth after cutting (hence diameter above in inches) were purchased from the British David Brown Co. in 1937. According to Japanese reports, the gears cut by the new machines were excellent and required little adjustment (in contrast to the gears cut using older machinery). At the same time, the modules of the Japan Standard Specification were revised: diametrical pitch was now set at 5.388 M5 (obliquity angle 14.5°) and M3.5 (obliquity angle 20°) instead of 7.00. There are indications that these new specifications were applied during the manufacture of the gearing for *Shōkaku*.

Turning Gear of the Main Engines

An electric and a manual turning unit to be fitted at one end of the pinion shaft of each LP turbine

4. Main Condensers

Each set of turbines to be equipped with a condenser with the following characteristics:

Cooling area:	1,387 m²
Length of tube sheet distance:	4,452 mm
Outer diameter of tubes:	16 mm
Thickness of tubes:	1.2 mm
Number of tubes:	6,200

5. Shaft Connections and Propellers

Table 7 Shaft dimensions

	Outer diameter	Inner diameter	Length inboard shaft	Length outboard shaft
	(mm)	(mm)	(mm)	(mm)
Thrust shaft	490	370	6,900	9,900
No. 1 intermediate shaft	490	370	6,600	5,900
No. 2 intermediate shaft	490	370	9,500	7,800
No. 3 intermediate shaft	490	370	–	9,500
Stern shaft	510	390	13,600	12,700
Propeller shaft	540	410	18,390	18,390

Thrust Shaft Bearing

Propeller thrust bearing to be of the Michell type, and the thrust shall not exceed 20 kg/cm² on the white alloy pad.

Brake

The claw brake shall be installed at the junction of the intermediate shaft and the stern shaft and has to hold the shaft at ¾ of the specified full-power torque.

Propellers

The dimensions shall conform to

Diameter:	4,200 mm
Pitch:	4,400 mm (approx.)
Developed area:	11.77 m² (approx.)[19]

6. Boilers

Eight boilers to be located in eight boiler rooms, which shall be of the open type. The specifications for the Kampon type model B oil-burning boilers shall be as follows:

Steam pressure:		30 kg/cm²
Steam temperature:		350°C
Temperature of preheated air:		135°C
Heating surface	evaporator tubes:	903 m²
	superheater tubes:	182 m²
	air preheater tubes:	454 m²
Volume, combustion space:		43.4 m³
Planned rate of combustion:		7.8 kg/m²
Atomizers:		Eight Kampon type 20 burners, model 3 Two Kampon type 20 burners, model 5
Cones:		Ten Kampon type 110 cone, model 5
Smoke screen ejector:		One of 2,000 kg/hr. capacity

7. Uptakes and Funnels

There shall be two funnels, the forward one to serve the forward group of four boilers, and the aft one the aft group. The funnels to be angled downward on the hull side. The specifications for the uptake and funnels areas for one boiler to be as follows:

Boiler top:	4.33 m²
Uptake area above middle deck:	3.46 m²
Funnel:	3.03 m²

8. Auxiliary Machinery

The types and numbers shall be as follows:

Table 8 Auxiliary Machinery		
In engine rooms	Type	Number
Circulating pump	Vertical, axial flow, turbo-reduction gear	4
Condensate pump	Horizontal, centrifugal, turbo-reduction gear drive	8
Lubrication oil pump	Vertical, gear type, turbo-reduction gear drive	8
Cooling-water pump	Vertical, axial flow, turbo-reduction gear drive	4
Air ejector	Dual stage, triplex, injection type	8
Supply ventilation	Horizontal, axial flow, turbo-reduction gear drive	4
Supply ventilation	Horizontal, axial flow, electric drive	4
Exhaust ventilation	Horizontal, axial flow, turbo-reduction gear drive	4
Exhaust ventilation	Horizontal, axial flow, electric drive	4
Control room ventilation	Horizontal, electric drive, "Sirocco" type	5
Fire and bilge pump	Vertical, electric drive, centrifugal	4
Portable heavy oil pump	Horizontal, gear, electric drive	1
Evaporator	Centrifugal, tube with thermo compressor	4
Distiller	Vertical, direct (surface) heating	2
Distiller pump	Horizontal, axial flow, turbo-reduction gear drive	4
Feed water heater	Vertical, direct (surface) heating	4
Oil cooler	Vertical, internal oil, external water	4
Oil purifier	Vertical, electric drive, centrifugal	2
Auxiliary condenser	*Shokkyoku* (?) type	2
Auxiliary water-circulating pump	Vertical, electric drive, centrifugal	2
In boiler rooms		
Main feed pump	Horizontal, axial flow, turbo-reduction gear	8
Auxiliary feed pump	Weir HD 8	8
Blower	Inverted, axial flow, turbo-reduction gear	6
Fuel oil service pump	Vertical, turbo-reduction gear	8
Fire and bilge pump	Vertical, electric drive	2
Auxiliary fuel oil service pump	Horizontal, electric drive, gear type	2
Auxiliary blower	Horizontal, electric drive, "Sirocco" type	2
Lubrication-oil-cooling pump	Horizontal, turbo-reduction gear combine pump; oil gear, water centrifugal	8
Oil cooler	Vertical, internal water, external oil	8
Feed water heater	Vertical, direct (surface) heating	8
Fuel oil heater	Vertical vent tube type	8
Blower for control room	Horizontal, electric drive, "Sirocco" type	8
Outside the machinery spaces		
Smoke-cooling pump	Horizontal, electric drive, centrifugal	2
Smoke ejector pump	Horizontal, electric drive, Elmo type	2
Fuel-oil-distributing pump	Horizontal, electric drive	3 (2 fwd, 1 aft)
Supply vent for machine shop	Horizontal, axial flow, electric drive	1
Exhaust vent for machine shop	Horizontal, axial flow, electric drive	1
Fore anchor windlass	Electric drive with gearing	1 set
Aft anchor windlass	Electric drive with gearing	1
Main steering gear	Electric drive, hydraulic	1 set
Auxiliary steering gear	Electric drive, hydraulic	1

9. Repair Facilities

The repair shop to be accommodated depending on aircraft carrier standard (battleship type)

10. Engine Weight
The estimated weight of engines is as follows:

Main engines:	675 metric tons
Shafting and propellers:	360 metric tons
Auxiliary machinery:	290 metric tons
Boilers and accessory equipment:	545 metric tons
Uptake and funnel installations:	120 metric tons
Pipes, cocks, valves, etc.:	360 metric tons
Miscellaneous:	185 metric tons
Water (trial condition):	250 metric tons
Total (without water):	2,535 metric tons
Total (with water at trial condition):	2,785 metric tons

In June 1941, *Shōkaku* attained 34.37 knots at 30,003 metric tons, 161,290 shp, and 307 shaft rpm. The effective horsepower (ehp) was calculated as 76,000 with a propulsion coefficient of 0.475, slightly in excess of the average value for carriers and identical to that of *Sōryū*. *Shōkaku*'s sister, *Zuikaku*, was slightly faster: 34.58 knots with 168,100 shp.

With the cruise turbines running at "allowable maximum power" (50,000 shp), speed was 26 knots, sufficient to obtain the speed of 13 m/sec. wind over deck necessary for aircraft takeoff in calm conditions. Note the huge increase in output between maximum cruise speed and maximum speed: more than 110,000 shp was required to increase speed from 26 knots to 34.5 knots. A total of 5,000 metric tons of heavy oil was required to attain the required endurance of 9,700 nautical miles at 18 knots.

The bulbous bow and the stern configuration, with its twin rudders, were adopted following experiments conducted in the course of the design of the "super-battleships" of the Yamato class. The semibalanced main rudder had an area of 34.367 m^2 and was placed abaft the propellers. Forward of it was a balanced auxiliary rudder with a surface area of 11.995 m^2.

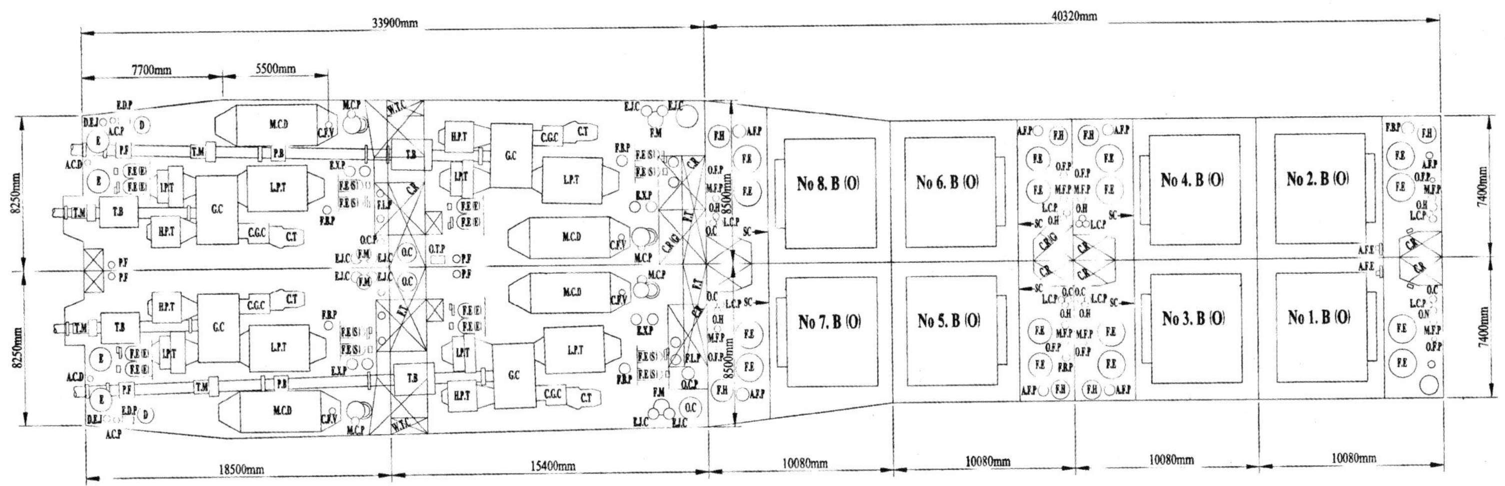

Layout of machinery spaces. Stern to the left, bow to the right. *From official plans*

Area of engine rooms (ER): 581 m²; area of boiler rooms (BR): 608 m²; horsepower/m² ER: 275.4; horsepower/m² BR: 263.2
Key: C.T. = cruise turbine; C.G.C. = cruise reduction gearing and coupling; G.C. = main gearing and coupling; H.P.T. = high-pressure turbine; I.P.T. = intermediate-pressure turbine; L.P.T. = low-pressure turbine; M.C.D. =main condenser; M.C.P. = main condensate pump

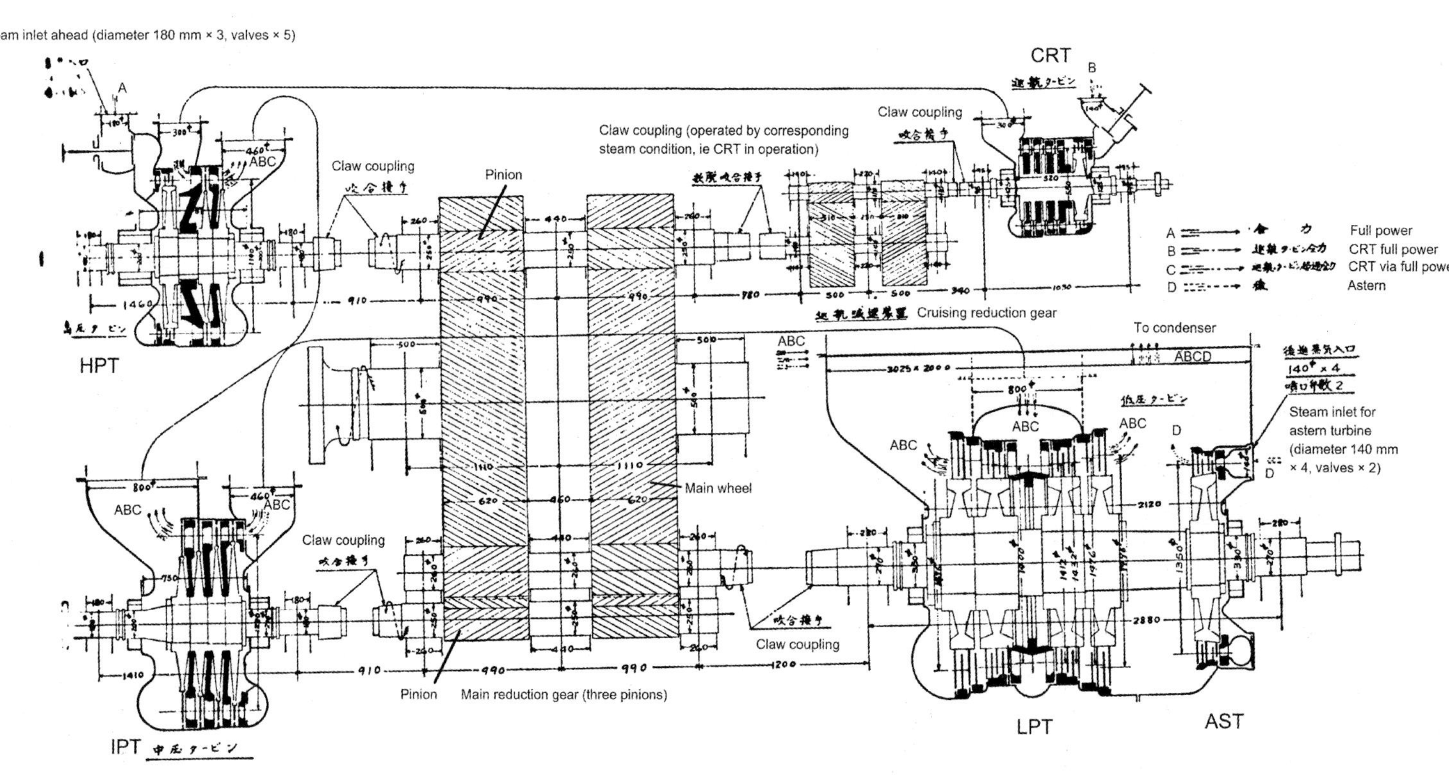

Layout of turbine set—port side forward. *Shōwa Zōsenshi*
Key: HPT = high-pressure turbine; IPT = intermediate-pressure turbine; LPT = low-pressure turbine; CRT = cruising turbine; AST = astern turbine

A view looking aft from *Zuikaku*'s bridge in the autumn of 1941. Thick black smoke is pouring from the funnels during an examination of engine performance. A covered 25 mm machine gun mount can be seen in front of the funnels, and to the right is part of the tripod signal mast. *Maruzen*

Zuikaku during exercises in the autumn of 1941. A torpedo bomber ("Kate") comes in to land, and the arrester wires are raised. Seawater is being sprayed on the funnel gases to reduce the exhaust temperature; hence the white smoke. Despite this, the cooled smoke was still hot enough to produce more steam when it hit the water surface.

CHAPTER 9

Armament

The antiaircraft armament of the Shōkaku class comprised eight type 89 40 cal., 12.7 cm twin high-angle gun mountings. They were divided into four groups, and for each group one type 94 high-angle fire control system was mounted. Gun mountings firing across the flight deck could engage targets on the opposite side down to only +12°. The mountings to starboard were numbered using odd numbers (1–7) from fore to aft, while those on the port side had even numbers (2–8). The two aft mountings to starboard (nos. 5 and 7) had shields to protect the crews against smoke and gases from the funnels. Ammunition provision was 250 rounds per gun plus twelve training rounds (*nendo jō*).

For close-range antiaircraft defense there were twelve type 96 25 mm triple machine guns: six to port, and six to starboard. Each pair of machine gun mountings had its own type 95 fire control director. As with the 12.7 cm mountings, the two mountings to starboard abaft the funnels had shields. The mountings to starboard were numbered using odd numbers (1–11) from fore to aft, while those on the port side had even numbers (2–12). Ammunition provision was 2,600 rounds for each 25 mm mounting, plus 100 training rounds.

The antiaircraft armament was stronger than that of the much-bigger carriers *Akagi* and *Kaga*, and the mounting of four type 94 high-angle fire control systems and six type 95 machine gun fire directors for remote fire control deserves particular attention. During the war, radar was fitted, the number of machine guns was increased, new types of aircraft were embarked, etc. Despite this, the IJN failed to keep pace with the rapid technical development on the Allied side.

Lack of space prevents detailed descriptions. However, the bulk of further equipment is enumerated below.

Table 9 Aircraft, Armament, and Other Equipment	
Aircraft and aviation equipment	
Type 0 fighter ("Zero")	18 (+2)
Type 99 dive-bomber ("Val")	27 (+5)
Type 97 torpedo bomber ("Kate")	27 (+5)
Arrester wire type, Kure model 4, modification 2	10
Crash barrier type, *Kūshō* model 3, modification 1 (fixed)	3
Aircraft elevator	3
Bomb elevators	2
No. 80 (800 kg) bomb	90
No. 25 (250 kg) bomb	306
No. 6 (60 kg) bomb	540
Catapult (planned)	1 set
Armament and associated equipment	
Type 89 40 cal., 12.7 cm HAG in twin mounting (250/12 rounds per gun)	8
Type 96 25 mm MG in triple mounting (2,600/100 rounds per gun)	12
12.7 cm ammunition hoist (vertical)	16
MG ammunition hoist (vertical)	16
MG ammunition hoist (horizontal)	1
Type 94 HA fire control system	4
Type 95 MG fire director	6
Training gun	2 sets
Type 14 6 m duplex rangefinder	2
Antigas system	1 set
Rifles and pistols	1 set

Torpedo equipment	
Kampon-type air compressor pump model 3, modification 1	5
Type 94 oxygen generator (planned)	1
Type 94 oxygen compressor (planned)	1
Compressed air flasks, type 2	8
Special oxygen flasks, type 2, modification 1	5
Small-type paravane, model 1	2
Minesweeping gear, model 1	2
Model 2 bomb disposal chain, modification 1	13
Medium-sized minesweeping gear, model 1, modification 1	2
Type 95 depth charge, modification 1	6
Air torpedo type 91	45
Sonar type 91, no. 4	1
Other equipment	1 set
Navigation equipment	
Type 93 magnetic compass no. 3	1
Type 90 magnetic compass no. 3, modification 1	1
Armstrong-type gyro compass no. 3 (double type)	1
Type 90 magnetic compass no. 3	1
Type 90 depth meter, model 2, modification 1	1
Type 92 pitometer log no. 2, modification 1	1
Type 96 dead-reckoning tracer, model 1	1
Type 91 wind speed meter, modification 1	1
Type 92 wind direction meter, modification 1	3
Type 97 balloon, modification 1	1
Other	1 set
Optical equipment	
Type 94 4.5 m rangefinder (as part of the HA fire control system)	4
Type 96 1.5 m rangefinder (as part of the MG fire director)	3
Type 13 18 cm binoculars with direction indicator	2
Type 13 HA 12 cm binoculars with direction transmitter and future setting	3
HA 12 cm binoculars (fixed on support)	2
Type 13 direction observation (bearing) plate, modification 1	4
Direction observation (bearing) plate (*mihari hōkōban*) for HA	4
Other equipment	1 set

Electrical equipment		
Main power supply (AC) composed of only generators		
AC turbo generator (each 600 kW, 225 V)		3
AC diesel generator (each 350 kW, 225 V)		2
Secondary power supply (DC) composed of generators and batteries		
Generator: 1 kW × 2, 50 kVA × 2, 20 kVA × 2, 3 kVA × 1, 6 kW x 1		
Battery: type 3, model 1 = 114 banks (1 set); same type 112 banks (4 sets)		
Type 96 110 cm searchlight, model 1		4
Type 96 searchlight director (controller)		4
60 cm signal searchlight		2
2 kW signaling light, modification 2		2
Other equipment		1 set
Radio equipment		
Transmitters	long wave, 500 W	2
	short and long wave, 500 W	1
	short wave, 500 W	4
	medium wave, 250 W	2
Receivers	long wave	3
	short and long wave	22
	short wave	2
Voice radio (wireless telephone)	medium wave	2
	short wave	1
	ultrashort wave, 5 kW	1
	ultrashort wave, 2 kW	2
	ultrashort wave, 1 kW	1
Radio direction finder, long and short waves		4
Wave meter, long-wave D/F instrument		1
	short-wave D/F instrument	2
	long-wave meter	4
	medium-wave meter	2
	short-wave meter	3
	ultrashort-wave meter	3
Wireless controller		4
Typewriter for decoding		4
Hydrophone (planned)		1

Notes

1. The list of weapons and equipment is as designed. There were numerous differences on completion. In particular, there were changes in the number and type of binoculars, and the oxygen compressors were suppressed (no oxygen-powered aerial torpedoes were embarked). The standard outfit of bombs was 60 × no. 80, 60 × no. 60, 312 × no. 25, 528 × no. 6, and 48 × no. 3; they were raised from the magazines to the hangar decks via one large and one small weapons lift. It is reported that nine torpedoes could be readied for operation simultaneously.
2. After the Battle for Midway, the number of fighters was increased from eighteen (+2) to twenty-seven (+5), while the number of dive-bombers embarked was reduced correspondingly. The original aircraft types were to have been replaced by newer models, but it was 1944 before new aircraft were embarked.
3. Each time *Shōkaku* was repaired following bomb damage, the number of 25 mm MG was increased. In May 1942, two triple mounts were added at the bow, two at the stern, and two forward and aft of the island, and in October an additional triple MG was mounted on the centerline between the two located at the bow and stern, making for a total of twenty triple mounts. Ten 25 mm single MG were added prior to the Battle of the Philippine Sea in June 1944. Following the loss of *Shōkaku* in that battle, *Zuikaku*'s close-range antiaircraft (AA) armament was again strengthened. She now had eight 12.7 cm twin HA mountings, twenty triple 25 mm mountings, twenty-six fixed single 25 mm, and ten transportable single 25 mm (total: 96 MG).
4. *Shōkaku* was the first IJN carrier to be equipped with radar. The antenna of the type 21 (air search), which had recently been accepted into service, was mounted atop the bridge between the end of August and early October 1942, and a second radar of the same type was added after October, the antenna taking the position of the former no. 3 110 cm retractable searchlight (mounted in a flight deck recess). When the first radar was mounted, the type 94 HA fire control system mounted atop the bridge was relocated to a newly constructed sponson to port, almost opposite the bridge. Prior to the Battle of the Philippine Sea (*A Gō Sakusen*) in June 1944, type 13 air search radar was also installed, with the antenna fixed to the light tripod mast abaft the island.
5. In August 1944, Kure Navy Yard mounted eight twenty-eight-tube rocket launchers on two newly built platforms similar to (but larger than) the MG sponsons. The launchers to starboard were located immediately forward of the forward HA guns. A fire control director was installed, and four rocket launchers were mounted in line. The length of the sponson was 12 m. The platform to port was located abaft the aft HA gun group; the fire control director and launchers were mounted in the same way as the starboard group. On forward and aft arcs the launchers could fire within 30° of the ship's axis. The 12 cm multiple rocket launcher and its projectile are described in *Warship* 34 (April 1985): 125–33, and in *Battleship Tosa Demolition Tests to the Modified Yamato Class* (Zagreb, Croatia: Despot Infinitus, 2019), 475–86.

Photo of 12.7 cm gun barrels (painted white) taken aboard a Shōkaku-class carrier probably after the Battle of Midway. *Gakken*

Firing scene of the 25 mm triple machine gun added aft of the signal mast aboard *Zuikaku*. It can be seen that there is no bulwark. Note also the scattered equipment, such as instrument boxes of unknown use. *Gakken*

A type 89 40 cal. 12.7 cm twin high-angle gun mount model A1. The Shōkaku class had six of this type plus two model A1 modification 2 with gas shields. For more information about this gun, and other guns, see this series' book *Sōryū, Hiryū, and Unryū-Class Aircraft Carriers*.

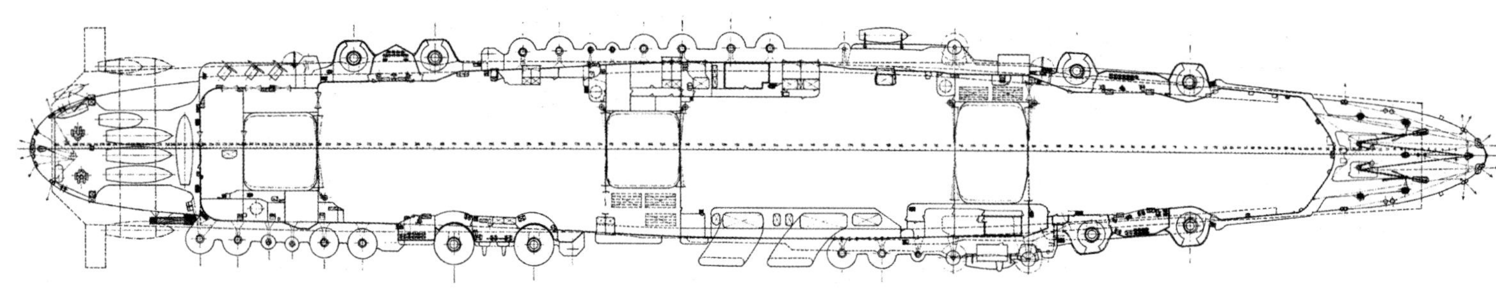

The high-angle gun deck (not an official term) and the upper hangar deck of *Shōkaku*. *Michael Wünschmann*

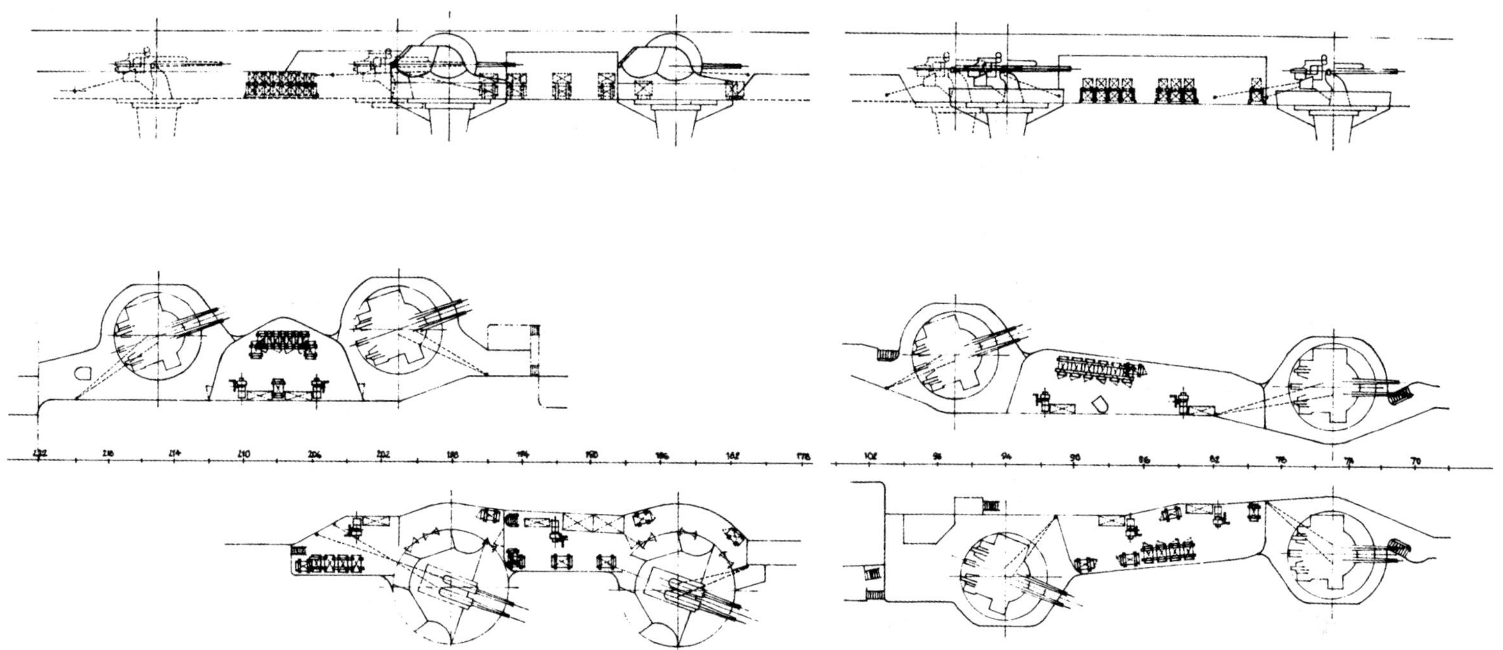

Arrangement of high-angle guns aboard *Shōkaku. Michael Wünschmann*

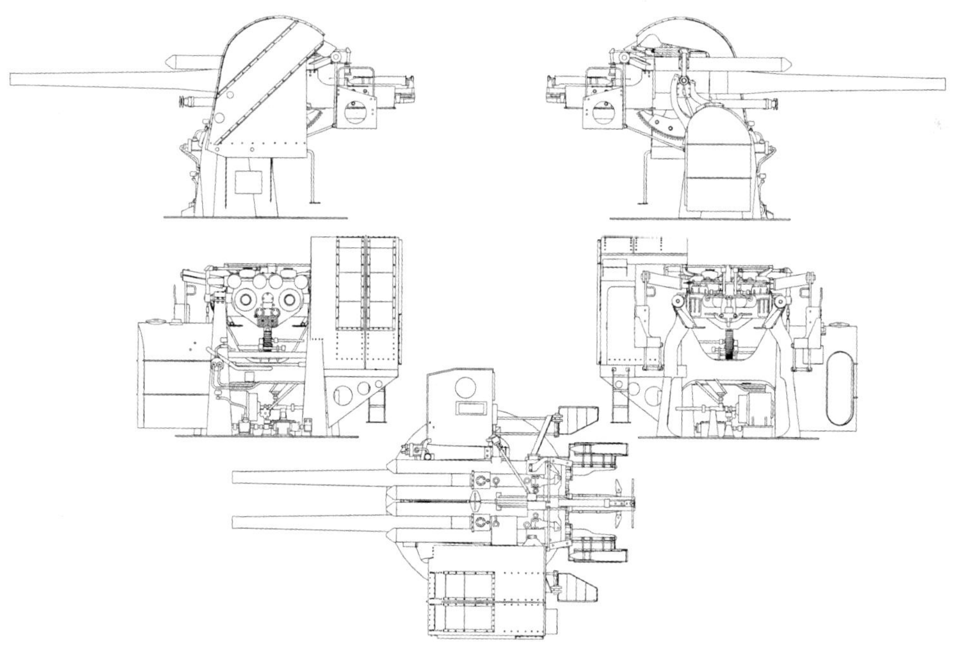

Plan and profile of type 89 40 cal. 12.7 cm twin high-angle gun model A1. *Waldemar Trojca*

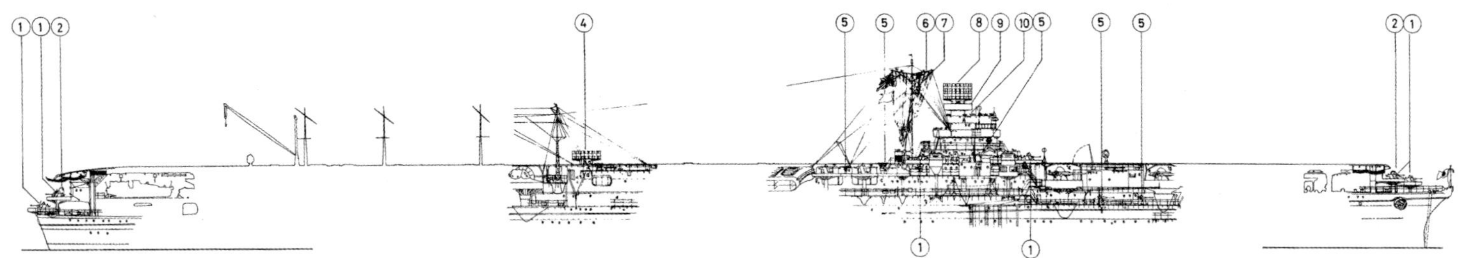

Armament changes of *Shōkaku* during the war—profile. *Michael Wünschmann*

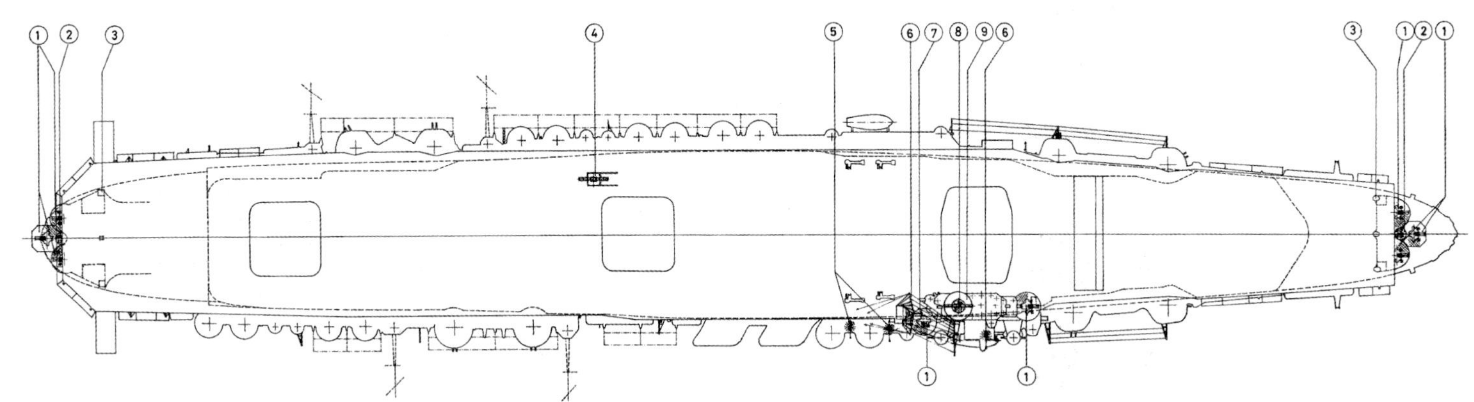

Armament changes of *Shōkaku* during the war—plan view. *Michael Wünschmann*
Key: 1 = type 96 25 mm triple machine guns; 2 = type 95 machine gun fire director; 3 = 25 mm portable single machine gun; 4 = mattress antenna of no. 21 air search radar; 5 = type 96 25 mm single machine gun; 6 = yard; 7 = antenna of no. 13 air search radar; 8 = mattress antenna of no. 21 air search radar; 9 = support for "8"; 10 = antiaircraft-defense open bridge with numerous binoculars

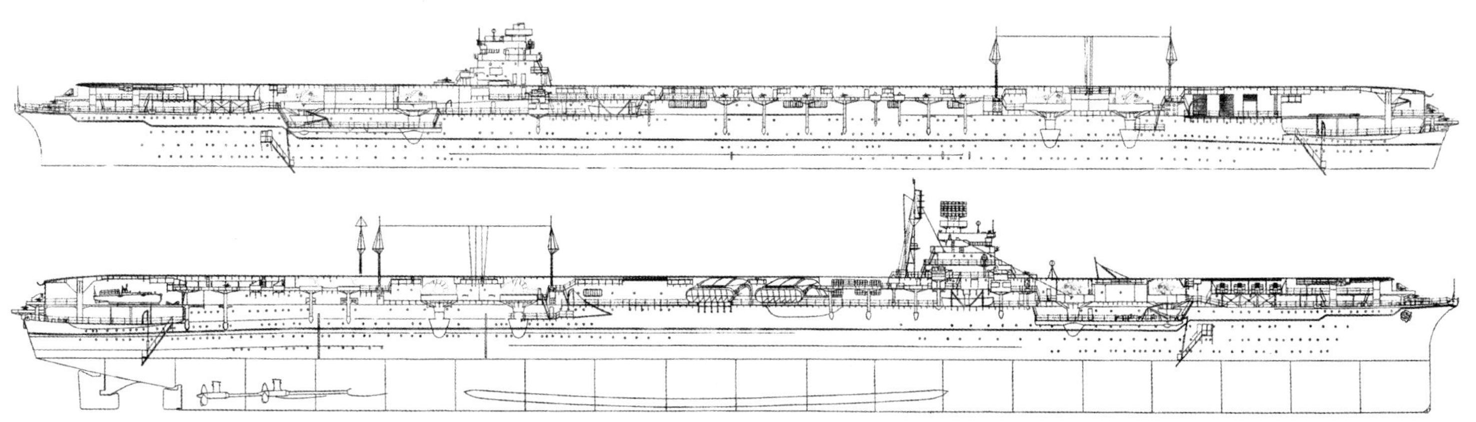

Profile of *Zuikaku* in 1944. *Michael Wünschmann*

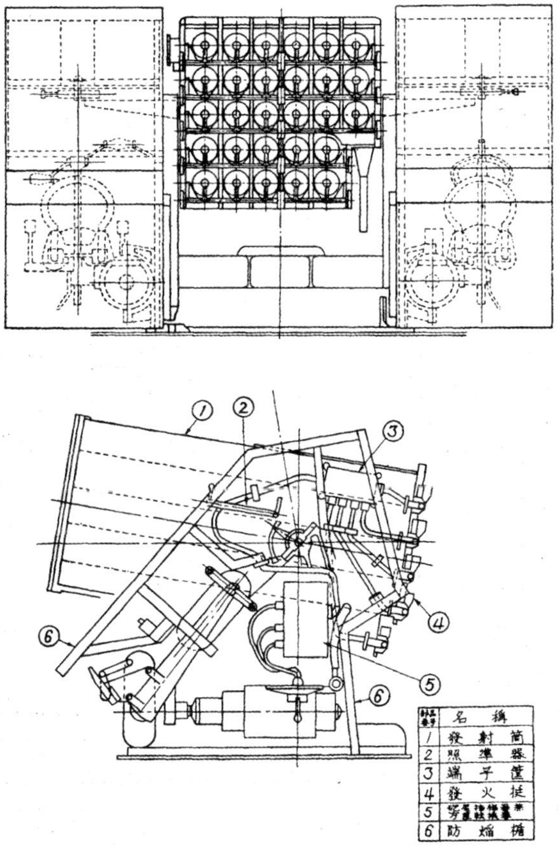

[illegible]	名稱
1	發射筒
2	照準器
3	端子筐
4	發火挺
5	[illegible]
6	防焔楯

Profile of 12 cm 28 tube rocket launcher *Sekai no Kansen*
Key: (1) Tubes; (2) Sight rest; (3) Terminal box; (4) Firing pin; (5) Combination breech cut-off and selector switch (for direct firing); (6) Flame shield.

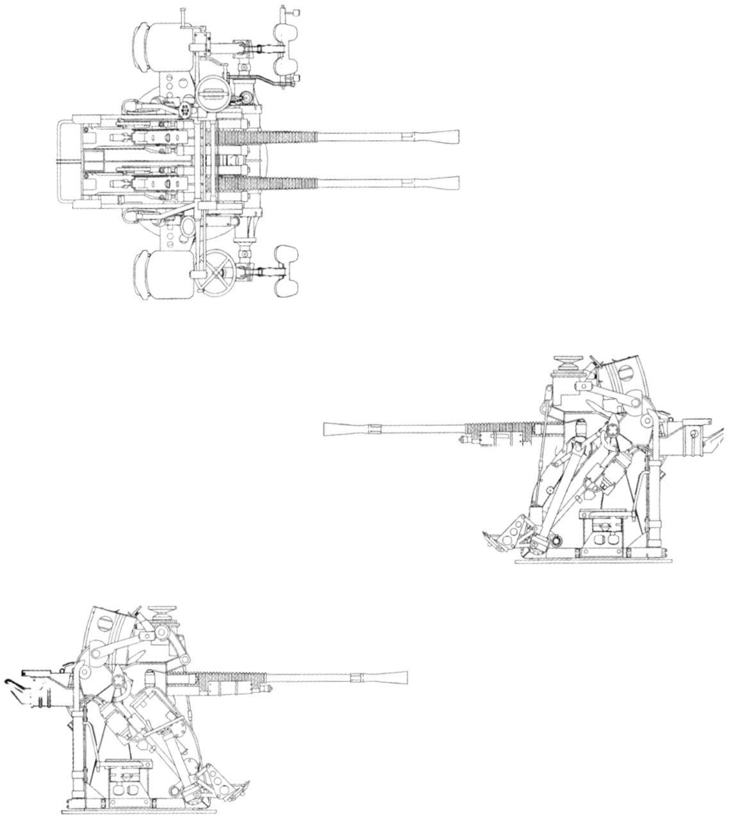

Plan and profile of type 96 25 mm twin machine gun mount. *Waldemar Trojca*

A photo taken at the end of November 1941. It shows *Zuikaku*, in the foreground, following the aircraft carriers *Kaga* and *Akagi* (barely visible) en route to Hawaii. Note the different island positions of *Kaga* (starboard) and *Akagi* (port). The Shōkaku class was designed with the position of the island bridge structure to port, but this was revised during the construction. This revision affected the smoke passages from the boilers, and *Shōkaku* had to have some patch-up work in the upper part of the hull. Note the windscreen in the recess in the flight deck (the sheet steel plate with numerous holes), the steel strip along the edge of the flight deck, the expansion joint, and the centerline marking with various angled lines (forward). To the left is the direction-finding loop antenna, and to the right, in the "pocket," a bench for the aircraft-handing personnel. On the foremost part of the flight deck are horizontal crew safety nets. Two twin 12.7 cm high-angle gun mounts (nos. 1 and 3), with steel bars fitted in order to prevent them from firing in "dangerous" directions, are also seen. On the flight deck the gun positions are marked with red and white paint.

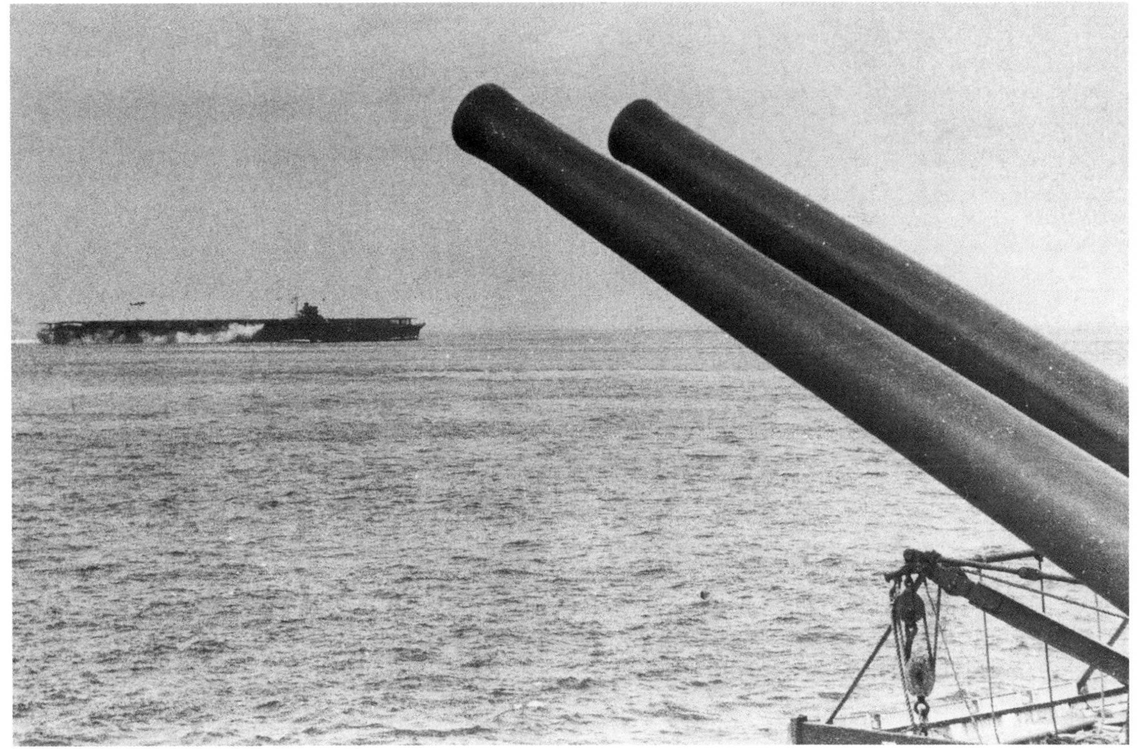

Zuikaku during flight training in the vicinity of Bungo Channel, probably on the morning of October 20, 1941. The photo is taken from the battleship *Mutsu*. The gun barrels in the foreground belong to a twin 12.7 cm, high-angle gun mount aboard *Mutsu*. *Sekai no Kansen*

The date and place of this photo are something of a mystery. At least one source suggests that it is showing *Zuikaku* at Truk at the end of October 1942, and that the photo should be from *Shōkaku*. However, this seems unlikely. A more recent study has suggested that it is *Zuikaku* in a photo probably taken from the port forward 12.7 cm, high-angle gun mount aboard *Hiryū*, and that the location could be Garreru anchorage in the Palau Islands on February 8 or 9, 1942.

Captain Nomoto Tameki is standing in front of *Zuikaku's* bridge structure. Captain Nomoto was *Zuikaku's* second commanding officer, and his term lasted from June 5, 1942, until June 20, 1943. A 1.5 m rangefinder can be seen on the lower bridge deck behind Captain Nomoto, and a triple 25 mm machine gun mount has been added. *Gakken*

A photo aboard *Shōkaku* taken during the launch of the second wave against Pearl Harbor on December 7, 1941. After instructions, the gathered flight crews, upon the command "All crews move!" ("*Sōin kakare*!"), rush to their planes. *Nihon Kaigun Kōkūtai Senjō Shashinshū*

A model 21 "Zero" is undergoing launch preparation aboard *Shōkaku* in early 1942. Maintenance personnel (*seibiin*) are attached to each wheel chock (*sharin-dome*), and they are waiting for the signal to remove them (*hazuse*). "EI-120" in the foreground has a drop tank attached below. These were reused, and that is why this one has dents in the surface. *Nihon Kaigun Kōkūtai Senjō Shashinshū*

Zuikaku prepares to launch a strike against Colombo on April 5, 1942. This probably shows planes getting ready for the second attack, and thirty-six planes are spotted, with "Zero" fighters in the front and "Val" dive-bombers behind. No bombs are hung under the dive-bombers. The wake reveals that the ship is turning into the wind.

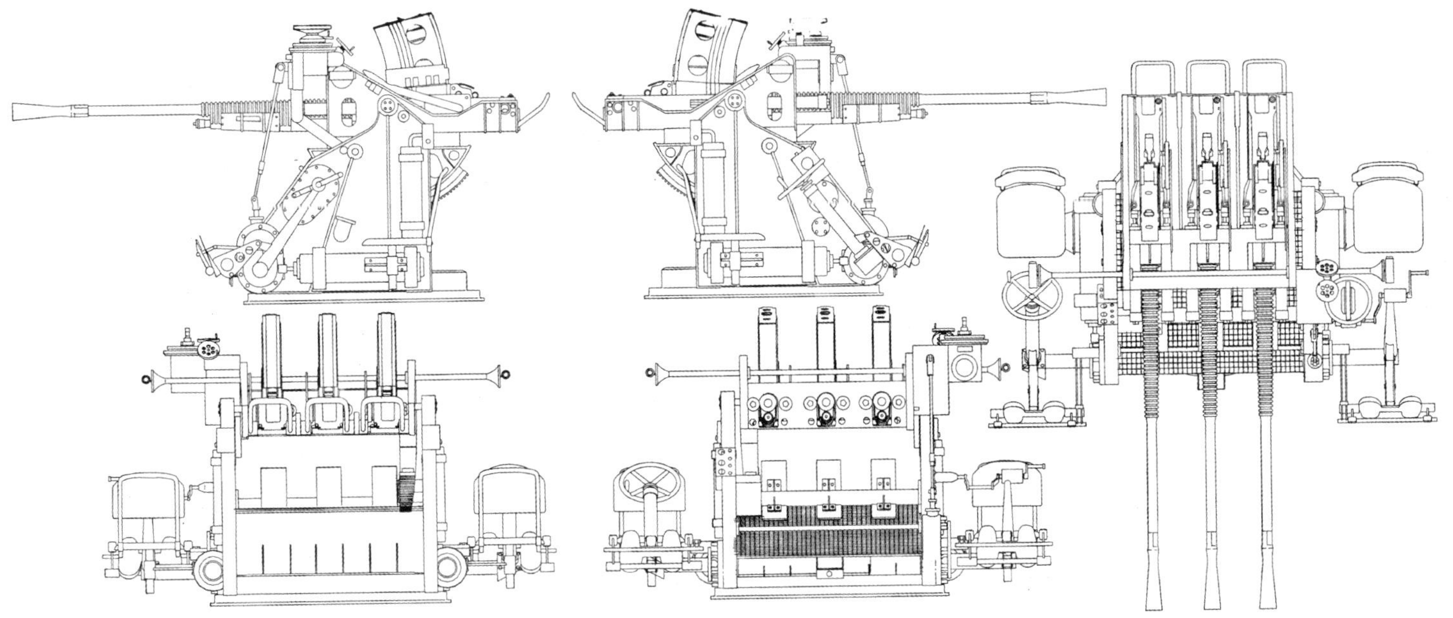

Plan and profile of type 96 25 mm triple machine gun mount. *Waldemar Trojca*

Planes waiting on the flight deck of *Zuikaku* on May 5, 1942, during the Battle of the Coral Sea. At the front are "Zero" fighters, and behind them "Val" dive-bombers. White canvas covers most of the planes in order to protect them from the tropical sunlight, and crew members are resting in the shade. The two planes in front are ready for takeoff at short notice.

At the Battle of Santa Cruz, *Shōkaku* is ready to launch an airstrike on October 26, 1942. As was common, the "Zero" fighters are up front, with the "Val" dive-bombers behind. Flight deck crew members are holding the wheel chocks, and they are waiting for the launch signal from the bridge.

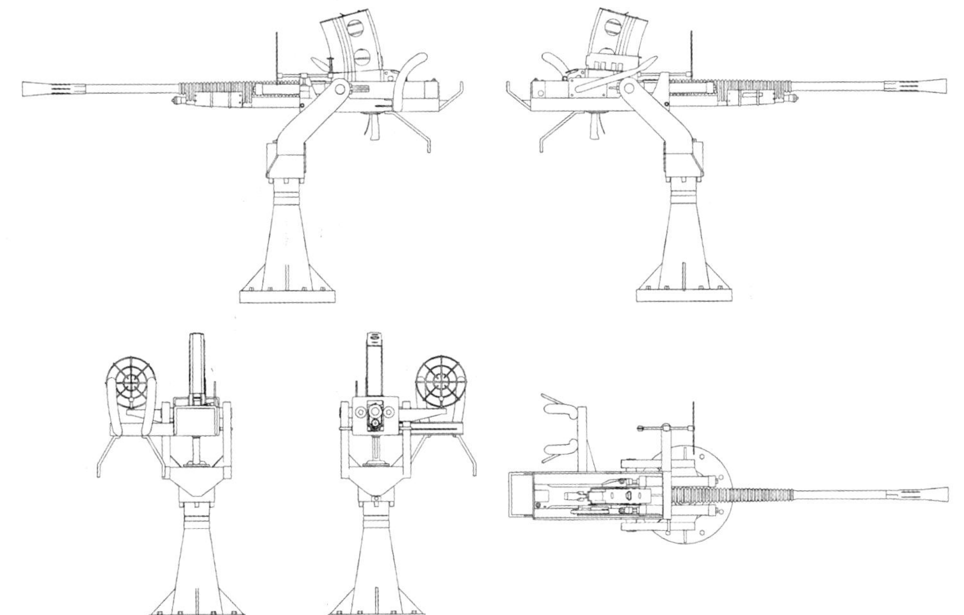

Plan and profile of type 96 25 mm single machine gun mount. *Waldemar Trojca*

CHAPTER 10

Complement

The planned complement was seventy-five commissioned officers, fifty-six special-service officers, seventy-one warrant officers, and 1,458 petty officers and ratings, for a total of 1,660 officers and men. Directive 1038 of December 27, 1939, with additional data dated June 30, 1943, lists the complement as seventy-five officers, fifty-six special-service officers, seventy-one warrant officers, 434 petty officers, and 1,026 ratings, for a total of 1,662. These figures were undoubtedly increased during the war with the fitting of additional antiaircraft guns, radar, and rocket launchers, but reliable data are lacking.

Officers of the *Zuikaku* photographed by the bridge structure in 1943. Captain Nomoto Tameki is sitting in the front row, eighth from the left. Behind the group is a large blackboard. *Gakken*

Shōkaku's gun room officers photographed on March 11, 1942. This photo is from a book by the ship's surgeon, Lieutenant Watanabe Naohiro, and he is standing in the back row, third from left. On the lower bridge deck, just above Watanabe's head, is located the searchlight controllers and the air watch direction panel. On the flight deck to the right can be seen part of the perforated edge plate that surrounded the middle elevator. *Kaisen, Kūbo Shōkaku*

At Truk on January 28, 1943, the crew of *Zuikaku* enjoys a performance by a comfort team from Tokyo on a special stage erected in the hangar. *Gakken*

A comfort team visits *Zuikaku* at Truk. In the center is Captain Nomoto Tameki (commanding officer), to the left is Commander Mitsui Masayoshi (executive officer), and to the right is Nomoto's adjutant, Okazaki. *Gakken*

A snapshot from *Zuikaku* at the end of 1942, as the crew is making preparations for the celebration of the new year. *Gakken*

CHAPTER 11

Operational Histories

Shōkaku

On August 25, 1941, incorporated into 1st Air Fleet (*Dai 1 Kōkū Kantai*), flagship 5th Carrier Division (*Dai 5 Kōkū Sentai*), commanded by RAdm. Hara Chūichi. December 7, 1941: Pearl Harbor attack. January 20, 1942: Rabaul attack, followed by New Guinea air raids. March 7–16, 1942: search for US Task Force 16. March–April 1942: operated in the Bay of Bengal and participated in the sinking of HMS *Hermes*. May 7–8, 1942: Battle of the Coral Sea and participated in the sinking of USS *Lexington*, USS *Sims*, and USS *Neosho*. Damaged by two bomb hits and under repair at Kure in May–June 1942. July 14, 1942: incorporated into 3rd Fleet (*Dai 3 Kantai*), 1st Carrier Division, commanded by VAdm. Nagumo Chūichi. August 24, 1942: Battle of the Eastern Solomons. October 26, 1942: Battle of Santa Cruz and participated in the sinking of USS *Hornet*. Damaged by four to six bomb hits and repaired at Yokosuka from November 1942 to February 1943. Sunk at 14:01 (11°50'N, 137°57'E) on June 19, 1944, at the Battle of the Philippine Sea, after being hit by three torpedoes from USS *Cavalla*, taking with her fifty-eight officers, 830 petty officers and ratings, 376 members of Air Group 601, and eight civilians (in total, 1,272). Removed from register on August 31, 1945.

Table 10 Commanding Officers, *Shōkaku*	
August 8, 1941	Jōjima Takatsugu
May 25, 1942	Arima Masafumi
February 16, 1943	Okada Tametsugu
November 17, 1943	Matsubara Hiroshi

Zuikaku

On November 14, 1941, incorporated into 1st Air Fleet (*Dai 1 Kōkū Kantai*), flagship 5th Carrier Division (*Dai 5 Kōkū Sentai*), commanded by RAdm. Hara Chūichi. December 7, 1941: Pearl Harbor attack. January 20, 1942: Rabaul attack, followed by New Guinea air raids. March 7–16, 1942: search for US Task Force 16. March–April 1942: operated in the Bay of Bengal and participated in the sinking of HMS *Hermes*. May 7–8, 1942: Battle of the Coral Sea and participated in the sinking of USS *Lexington*, USS *Sims*, and USS *Neosho*. July 14, 1942: incorporated into 3rd Fleet (*Dai 3 Kantai*), 1st Carrier Division. August 24, 1942: Battle of the Eastern Solomons. October 26, 1942: Battle of Santa Cruz and participated in the sinking of USS *Hornet*. April 1, 1943: flagship 3rd Fleet (VAdm. Ozawa Jisaburō). April 1, 1944: no longer flagship. June 18–20, 1944: Battle of the Philippine Sea. August 15, 1944: incorporated into 3rd Fleet, 3rd Carrier Division. Sunk at 14:14 (19°20'N, 125°20'E) on October 25, 1944, at the Battle of Cape Engaño, after being hit by several bombs and torpedoes, taking with her forty-nine officers (including her CO) and 794 petty officers and ratings (in total 843). Removed from register on August 31, 1945.

Table 11 Commanding Officers, *Zuikaku*	
September 25, 1941	Yokokawa Ichihei
June 5, 1942	Nomoto Tameki
June 20, 1943	Kikuchi Tomozō
December 18, 1943	Kaizuka Takeo

Zuikaku follows the aircraft carrier *Kaga* and *Akagi* at the end of November as the force was about to attack Pearl Harbor. Note the different island positions of *Kaga* (starboard) and *Akagi* (port). The Shōkaku class was designed with the position of the island bridge structure to port, but this was revised during the construction. This revision affected the smoke passages from the boilers, and *Shōkaku* had to have some patch-up work done in the upper part of the hull.

A type 97 ("Kate") torpedo bomber takes off from *Zuikaku* for the second wave of the attack on Pearl Harbor on December 7, 1941. The crew members swing their caps (*bōure*) and cheer, "*Banzai*!" This photo was released by the IJN and was published in numerous books.

On January 20, 1942, a "Zero" fighter model 21 takes off from *Zuikaku* for the attack on Rabaul. At this time, *Zuikaku*'s planes could be identified by the red letters "EII" on the fin and the two white bands around the fuselage. *Shōkaku*'s had "EI" and one white band.

Photo taken from *Shōkaku* (note the 25 mm machine gun mount in the foreground) showing Vice Admiral Nagumo Chūichi's striking force in the Indian Ocean in March 1942. *Zuikaku* is immediately ahead of *Shōkaku*, and beyond can be seen (*from the right*) the battleships *Kongō*, *Haruna, Kirishima, and Hiei* and the aircraft carriers *Hiryū*, *Sōryū*, and *Akagi*.

The first day of the Battle of the Coral Sea on May 7, 1942. The 5th Carrier Division, with *Shōkaku* and *Zuikaku*, are photographed from the heavy cruiser *Haguro*. A screening destroyer can be seen to the right. *The Maru Special*

A torpedo-armed type 97 torpedo bomber ("Kate") takes off from *Zuikaku* at the Battle of the Coral Sea. Because of the weight of the torpedo, the takeoff run needed almost the full length of the flight deck. Note the many crew members in the "pockets" waving and cheering. In the foreground the three wires of two crash barriers can be seen, followed by the cover of an expansion joint and then a row of arrester wires. The radio masts are in lowered position.

Shōkaku under air attack by US torpedo planes and dive-bombers during Operation "MO" (the occupation of Port Moresby)—the Battle of the Coral Sea—early on May 8, 1942. Note the high water geysers caused by bombs.

Shōkaku maneuvers violently to avoid being hit, and here she appears to be maneuvering with maximum helm angle and at 8/10 speed.

Shōkaku under attack on May 8, 1942. The white spot forward marks a hit at that position. The bomb penetrated the forward part of the flight deck and detonated on the anchor deck. Fires erupted, and the anchors went to the bottom.

Photo taken on May 8, 1942, of the forward port side of *Shōkaku's* buckled flight deck, caused by the bomb hit forward. "A" marks the hitting point. Note the white markings on the flight deck. Takeoff and landing were along the centerline, and the radially arranged white markings (each angled 10°) indicate the wind direction above the steam pipe placed on the centerline forward. *Kure Maritime Museum*

The starboard side of *Shōkaku's* buckled and torn anchor deck on May 8. Note the antiskid measures taken by small steel sheets welded onto the deck. The same arrangement was used at the forward and aft parts of the flight deck, where no wood was used. *Kure Maritime Museum*

The forward aircraft elevator on *Shōkaku* jammed due to the shock. It could not be moved, and aircraft could not be operated. Note the platform, the surrounding perforated sheet metal, and the planks used on the flight deck. This photo was taken on May 8. *Kure Maritime Museum*

Shōkaku entered Kure Navy Yard in the evening of May 17 for repairs, and a series of photos were taken shortly after that. Wooden patches seen in the photos were part of urgent repairs made by the crew. This photo shows the port side, with the damaged anchor deck and flight deck. At this time, the damage inspection was still in full swing. The bow is to the left, outside the photo margins, and in the foreground various equipment of the navy yard can be seen. The funnel seen to the right belongs to the steam boiler, partly seen on the lower right edge of the photo. *Kure Maritime Museum*

The port side of the anchor deck and flight deck taken from a different angle. The structure of the anchor deck can be seen in the center. Note the arrangement of the patches made by the crew to avoid flooding. *Kure Maritime Museum*

The boats were stored one upon another to save space. In this photo (May 8), a damaged 12 m diesel-powered launch is seen. Above is the gangway used when the ship was boarded at the stern. *Kure Maritime Museum*

The starboard side of the boat deck (on May 8), showing parts burned by the detonation and the subsequent fire. In contrast to the fire forward, it could soon be extinguished. On the left-side center (below the control station for the ship's boats), the bow of a boat (9 m cutter) can be seen. Below it, part of the gangway is visible. *Kure Maritime Museum*

Another photo of the damaged boat deck, taken on the same date. The sponson of the no. 11 triple 25 mm machine gun mount can be seen right above. The mount was completely destroyed, and all gunners were killed. *Kure Maritime Museum*

The second bomb hit the aft edge of the flight deck to starboard and detonated just below. Fire broke out, but it could be extinguished quicker than the fire in the forward part of the ship. The boat hangar was destroyed, and a large part of the boat deck was damaged. Splinters pierced every wall and bulkhead in the vicinity. Even the aft elevator was damaged, but it did not jam. One 25 mm triple machine gun mount was destroyed, and several compartments became unusable. This photo from May 8 shows the damage to the aft boat deck, with the hole in the flight deck. The splinter damage to the aft hangar wall is marked with white circles. The fence-like structure on the aft hangar wall below the flight deck is the equipment for lowering and hoisting of the ship's boats. *Kure Maritime Museum*

The third bomb hit at the side aft of the island structure and detonated outside the hull plating. The island was damaged by splinter and blast. One strut of the tripod signal mast was broken, two type 94 high-angle gun fire control systems to port and two 25 mm triple machine gun mounts on the starboard side sponsons were damaged, and the fire director for these machine guns was wrecked. The structure of the starboard side of the upper hangar was also damaged, and equipment in the vicinity of the detonation was destroyed. It is supposed that this bomb could have caused fatal damage had it detonated inside the hangar. This photo shows the island structure on May 8.

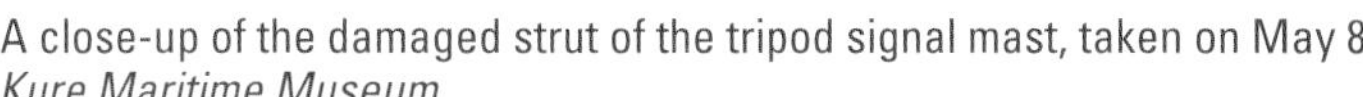
A close-up of the damaged strut of the tripod signal mast, taken on May 8. *Kure Maritime Museum*

This photo from May 8 was taken from the starboard side of the open bridge (antiaircraft defense station), looking aft. At the lower edge, part of the 4.5 m stereo, high-angle gun rangefinder of the type 94 high-angle fire control system is visible. Below it is the sponson, with the totally destroyed machine gun fire director, followed by the hole caused by penetration and detonation of the bomb. Farther aft (*above*) are two 25 mm triple machine gun mounts and their sponsons. Note the damage to the forward sponson. The damaged signal mast is to the right on this photo. *Kure Maritime Museum*

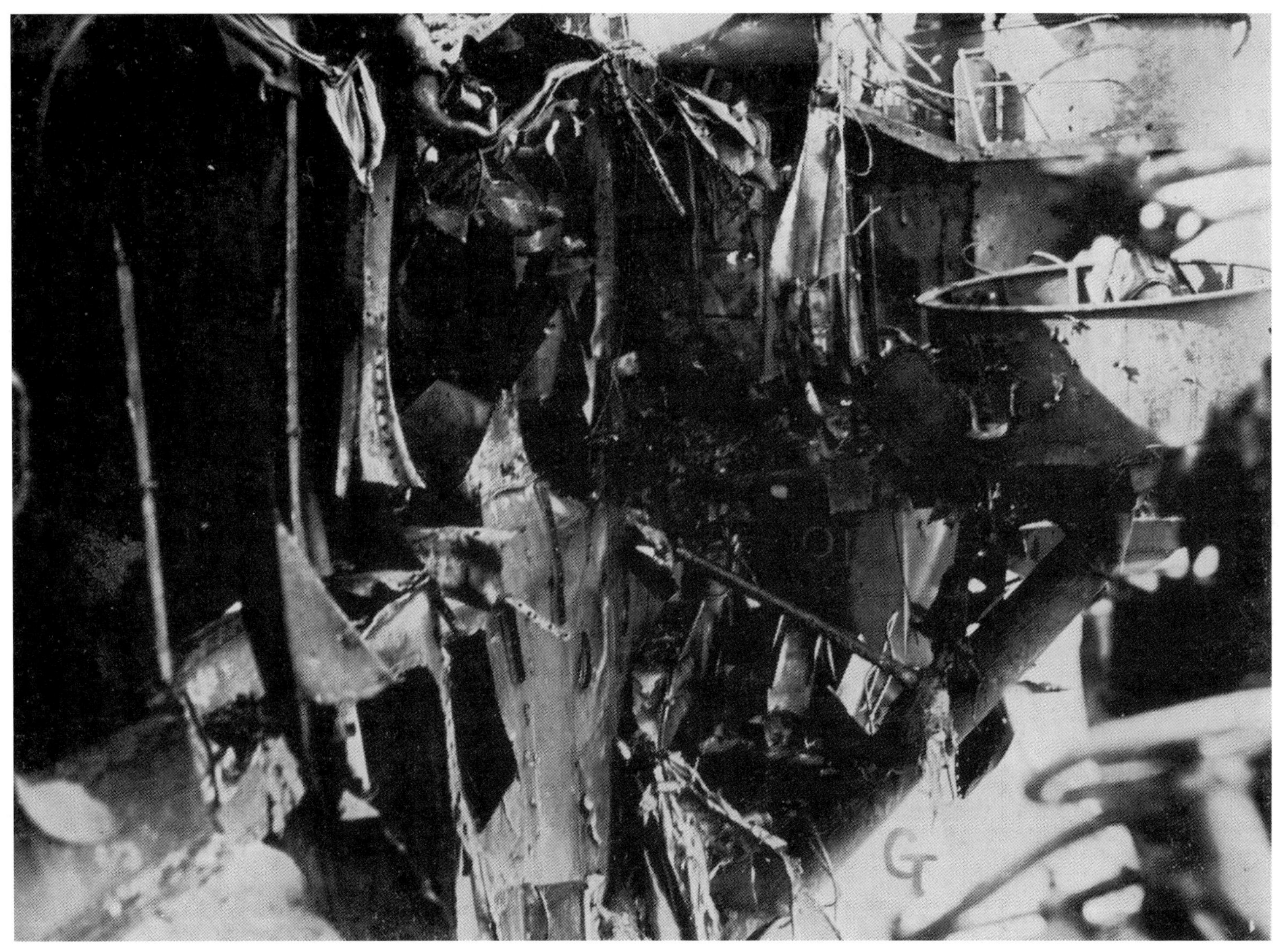

Damage to the starboard side of the hull below the bridge structure, shown on May 8. To the right (*a little above the center*) is the sponson of the destroyed machine gun fire director. The handling party was killed instantly and blown overboard. Only the finger (on the trigger) of the layer remained. *Kure Maritime Museum*

This photo is from a series of photos published during the war. They were taken from the anchor deck of *Shōkaku* and show *Zuikaku* in the autumn of 1942, about the time of the Battle of Santa Cruz. Machine guns have now been fitted below the forward edge of the flight deck. Note the plane that has just been launched. *Gakken*

Shōkaku or *Zuikaku* at high speed in the South Pacific in 1942. This photo is from a 16 mm film, and it is not certain if 25 mm machine guns are mounted forward, but a type 21 air-search radar can be seen mounted on top of the bridge. After the Battle of Midway, radar was regarded as essential. *The Maru Special*

Shōkaku in damaged condition at the Battle of Santa Cruz on October 26, 1942. She was attacked by US planes after launching her first and second attack groups, and bombs caused similar damage as at the Battle of the Coral Sea. All bombs hit the flight deck: one to starboard (frame 188) and three to port (middle elevator and flight deck at frames 195 and 214). The flight deck and both upper and lower hangars were damaged. This view from the bridge shows the buckled flight deck, caused by bombs detonating inside the hangar. Damage control parties are still trying to extinguish the fires. *Kure Maritime Museum*

Firefighters in action on *Shōkaku's* flight deck on October 26, 1942. A serious fire erupted, and the ship was in grave danger. Since firefighting had been improved after the Battle of Midway, the fires were extinguished after a hard fight. However, the middle elevator was seriously damaged, and the forward and aft elevators were deshaped. The buckled flight deck fell down amidships over a length of about 25 m. *Shōkaku* could no longer operate aircraft and retired to Truk escorted by the destroyers. *Kure Maritime Museum*

Photo taken at Truk on October 28, showing where the bombs actually hit *Shōkaku*'s flight deck. All bombs penetrated the flight deck and detonated in the hangar below. Aft, a B5N2 ("Kate") torpedo bomber that miraculously survived. "A" is the hit to port by the middle elevator, "B" caused great damage to the flight deck aft at frame 195, "C" shows the same at frame 214, and "D" is the damage at frame 188 (starboard).

A close-up of the damage caused by the hits to port. Two gun barrels of twin 12.7 cm, high-angle gun mount no. 6 can be seen (no. 8 is partly seen aft). The ability of the bombs to damage the thin wood-covered flight deck is obvious. There was also damage in the hangar below, and some eighty crew members were killed. This photo was taken on October 28, and in the background the heavy cruiser *Tone* enters Truk anchorage. *Kure Maritime Museum*

Shōkaku at Truk on October 28, showing damage to the 12.7 cm, high-angle guns (nos. 5 and 7) on the aft starboard side. These guns were completely destroyed, and all crew members in the vicinity were killed. Fortunately, the propulsion system remained undamaged. The person standing on the deck is the chief of the damage control party, Commander Fukuchi Kaneo. *Kure Maritime Museum*

A view of *Shōkaku*'s hangar, flight deck, and middle elevator as seen from the lower hangar deck on October 28. One can see the collapsed part of the flight deck, and the person in the center is Commandor Fukuchi Kaneo. Fukuchi was very lucky, because not only did he survive the carrier battles of 1942, but when he was then posted to the battleship *Mutsu*, he was erroneously diagnosed with an aortic aneurysm and was not aboard when *Mutsu* blew up. After the war he wrote several books, and he did not pass away until 1996, aged ninety-four. *Kure Maritime Museum*

The collapsed flight deck aft of the middle aircraft elevator. *Kure Maritime Museum*

View of the wrecked flight deck from the upper part of the hangar deck. *Kure Maritime Museum*

The wrecked flight deck forward of frame 195. The island bridge can be seen forward of the damage, but unfortunately the type 21 radar cannot be seen on this photo. *Kure Maritime Museum*

A view of the flight deck, looking aft. Two arrester wires can be seen, as well as an expansion joint with its cover steel plate. *Kure Maritime Museum*

Zuikaku with a deck load of planes. It is estimated that it was taken in 1943, but the location is uncertain.
Kure Maritime Museum

The 3rd Fleet anchored at Eniwetok on September 20–23, 1943. This photo was taken by a news team from *Asahi Shimbun* and shows *Zuikaku* with planes on her deck. The other ships shown are the heavy cruisers *Chikuma* (*left*), *Tone*, and probably *Haguro* (*right*).

Another photo of the commander in chief of the Combined Fleet, Admiral Koga Mineichi, and the commander of the 3rd Fleet, Vice Admiral Ozawa Jisaburō (*right*), conferring on the afterpart of *Zuikaku's* compass bridge deck sometime between August or October 1943. Part of the wind direction (*fūkō*) and wind force (*fūsoku*) receiver box can be seen beside Admiral Koga.

The aircraft carrier *Taihō* at Tawitawi anchorage (Borneo) on May 15–16, 1944. Beyond *Taihō* is an aircraft carrier of the Shōkaku class, and to the right the battleship *Nagato*. Note the small "tent" forward and the B6N (*Tenzan, "Jill"*) torpedo bombers on *Taihō*. This photo was found on Saipan by the American intelligence and was included in a US Navy identification booklet in October 1944. *National Archives*

The 1st Mobile Force (*Dai 1 Kidō Butai*) on June 15, 1944, during Operation "*A Gō*." This is a photo from the heavy cruiser *Maya*, and it shows the aircraft carrier *Taihō* (*left*), the battleship *Nagato* (*center*), and the aircraft carrier *Shōkaku* (*right*). The force departed Guimaras (Philippines) on June 15 and headed for the Battle of the Philippine Sea, where *Taihō* and *Shōkaku* were lost.

Zuikaku and two destroyers under air attack at the Battle of the Philippine Sea on June 20, 1944. Despite fierce attacks, only one bomb hit. It hit her just aft of the island structure and detonated in the upper hangar, and fires erupted in the hangar and on the flight deck. After some misunderstandings, the fires were brought under control and extinguished, and *Zuikaku* could proceed under her own power. This was *Zuikaku's* first battle damage. *US Navy*

On June 22, 1944, *Zuikaku* briefly stopped in Nakagusuku Bay, Okinawa, and she then returned to Hashirajima on June 24, when this photo was taken by Lieutenant j.g. Ishikawa Toshio. Although *Zuikaku* was not fatally damaged at the Battle of the Philippine Sea, the damage was still terrible, not least because of the splinters from countless near misses. Note the closed portholes and the degaussing cable. Fukui Shizuo writes that when he saw only one ship returning to port, he exclaimed, "One ship! Only one ship!" There was no trace of *Taihō* or a second Shōkaku-class carrier. *Kure Maritime Museum*

Zuikaku, with a destroyer, seen from above during exercises in the autumn of 1944. In this view it can be seen that the bridge structure is quite close to the bow. *Sekai no Kansen*

CHAPTER 12

Detailed Action Record (DAR) of the Aircraft Carrier Zuikaku from October 20 to 25, 1944[20]

Zuikaku Kimitsu* (secret) *Dai 12 Gō-11

I. Situation (omitted)

II. Planning

(1)
Tasks corresponding to *Kimitsu Kidōbutai* (Secret Mobile Force) Operational Order #76 (*Kidōbutai Shō Gō* Operation details)
(2)
Operation Preparations
On the basis of the lessons of *A Gō Sakusen* (operation), the following was carried out:
(A) Personnel replacement
(B) Increase of the weapons
Increase and additional machine gun and rocket gun mounts

Type 89 40 cal., 12.7 cm twin high-angle guns	8 (16 guns)
Type 96 triple machine guns	20 (60 guns)
Type 96 single machine guns	36 (36 guns)
28-barreled rocket guns (*funshin-hō*)	8 (224 barrels)
Type 92 7.7 mm movable machine guns	5

(C) Communications weapons
One radio D/F (*hōi-sokuteiki*) for medium wave and one for short wave, fitted before departure
The following were additionally fitted:
Two pairs T.M.-type short-wave, movable telegraphs (for type A short-wave regulation, one pair in reserve)
Two pairs T.M.-type short-wave, movable telegraphs (for types A and C short wave, GF general short-wave regulation)
Six pairs type 96 *Kū* no. 3 telegraphs (for types A and C short-wave and warning and GF general short-wave regulation)
Four pairs type I *Kū* no. 3 telephones within own force (communication between nos. 1 and 2 transmitting and nos. 1 and 2 receiving)
Two pairs type I *Kū* no. 3 telephones (communication within the Third Air Attack Force)
Two pairs type III *Kū* no. 1 telegraphs (communication between CAP [*jōkū-chokuei-kōgekiki-tai*])
(D) Electronic
Two type 13 radars newly installed
(E) Underwater weapons
Type 0 (*rei shiki*) hydrophone fitted
(F) Takeoff and landing areas
Supplementation of arrester gear and crash barrier installations
(G) New fitting of five air pumps (capacity 30 tons/hr., pressure 10 kg/cm^2 for drainage)
(H) Preparations for minimizing the extent of damage
(1) Execution of measures for minimizing damage by avgas
(a) Reinforcement of the protection of avgas tanks by filling the void spaces with iron concrete
(b) Exhaust of avgas vapor reinforced by two ventilators with 2 hp motors
(c) Ventilators for the exhaust of avgas vapor in the hangars refitted and increased:
Five units refitted to 18 hp, from 3 hp
Fifteen units of 3 hp increased
(2) Measures for the maintenance of buoyancy
Closure of nine water protection covers, nine manholes, two bulkheads
(3) Radical removal of combustible items
Aside from the items directly related to fighting, all others were landed or stored below the waterline

(4) Execution of measures for minimizing damage
All divisions carried out radical measures for minimizing damage by shells (rolled hammocks, sandbags, etc.)
Fire protection facilities
Distributed storage of emergency materials, reserve weapons, commodities
(5) Others
As food to be distributed before battle are loaded:
Various sorts of canned rice: two portions per man, 2,500 men
Dried rice: two portions per man, 2,500 men
(I) Training
The greater part of the complement were excellent sailors who participated in *A Gō Sakusen*. They were supplemented by other personnel during the stay at Kure and during the maintenance work. *Zuikaku* moved to the western part of the Inland Sea from Kure at the end of August to carry out special training. By rigorous training, a quick improvement prior to the great operation was intended. During this time, the official trial with the newly fitted equipment, landing training, air battle training, and antisubmarine warfare (ASW) training was carried out. Upon departure, the whole crew was eager to fight and filled with self-confidence to oppose the enemy.

(J) Items influencing the operation
Aircraft
The aircraft of the 3rd CarDiv are not the own 653rd Air Group, but they belong to a mixed force established for emergency cases, remaining parts of base planes, and one part of the 601st Air Group. The departure prevented an opportunity for common training; the execution of the air attacks and such will be influenced considerably negatively.

Weather
Before entering the sea area of the decisive battle, the weather was generally not good. Visibility was bad and often prevented reconnaissance and observation. The weather cleared up on the 24th; however, the cloudiness was still 8 and influenced the search for the enemy.
On the morning of the 25th in the weather was good visibility 60,000 m; conditions for reconnaissance/lookout (for air battle) are good. In the afternoon, cloudiness 5–8; negative influence on the air battle is expected.

III Sequel

(1) Battle sequel
(a) General

Table 12: DAR, General	
Date/Weather/Time Battle sequel (own force) Friendly forces (battle sequel)	
October 20: Cloudy	
0600	Departed Ōita with all aircraft embarked
1400	Passed western part of the Inland Sea
1720	Hearing noise; crew alerted for battle
1735	Passed Bungo Strait. Fleet took first patrol formation in line; speed 18 knots. Condition inside the ship: reconnaissance first detainment
1755	ASW aircraft (seaplane) discovered an enemy submarine. Takeoff to suppress
1756	Speed 20 knots
1759	Hearing the noise of an enemy submarine in direction 130°
1828	Observed/heard electric wave 98 MC in direction 170°
1830	*Chitose* heard electric wave 110 MC in direction 110°
1902	Condition inside the ship: reconnaissance second detainment
2100	Condition inside the ship: patrol third detainment A method
October 21: Cloudy, sometimes drizzle	
0014	Speed 18 knots
0515	??
0545	Control of noise warning (gear)
0618	Speed 16 knots
0720	Takeoff of reconnaissance planes (fo × 6)
1152	Landing of reconnaissance planes (fo × 3)
1202	Heard noise of torpedo propellers, direction 220°; evading course, commenced fire to chase off the submarine
1219	Landing of reconnaissance planes (fo × 1)
1220	Condition inside the ship: patrol second detainment
1237	Landing of reconnaissance planes (fo × 1)
1345	Condition inside the ship: patrol third detainment A method
1435	Landing of reconnaissance planes (fo × 1)
October 22: Cloudy	
0420	Heard noise similar to diesel noise; ready for action, evading routing

0438	Condition inside the ship: patrol second detainment
0515	Ready for action; *Zuihō* discovers periscope in direction 200°
0520	Confirmed torpedo wake starboard 90°; rudder hard over position to avoid hit
0549	Takeoff of seven reconnaissance planes
0602	Condition inside the ship: patrol third detainment A method
1105	Takeoff of reconnaissance planes (fo × 2)
1153	Discovered torpedo wake in direction 40°; rudder hard over position to avoid hit
1156	Condition inside the ship: patrol second detainment
1210	Landing of one fo; greatly damaged
1239	Landing of two fo
1251	Speed 12 knots; beginning of the fleet supply
1300	Condition inside the ship: patrol third detainment A method
1537 (!)	Takeoff of two fo for ASW patrol
1515 (!)	Landing of two fo and one fb
1647	Landing of one fb
1746	Landing of two fo flown ASW patrol
2025	Speed 16 knots
2010	Light cruiser *Tama* discovers torpedo wakes, ready for action
2013	Torpedo wake at starboard; rudder hard over position to avoid hit
2017	Destroyer *Wakatsuki* approaches to suppress submarine
2025	Condition inside the ship: patrol second detainment
2100	Condition inside the ship: patrol third detainment A method
October 23: Cloudy	
0515	??
0531	Light cruiser *Isuzu* discovers enemy submarine; rudder hard over position to avoid hit
0545	Takeoff of reconnaissance planes (fo × 8)
0608	Landing of one fo
0611	Condition inside the ship: patrol third detainment A method
0632	Maximum battle speed, immediate "maintenance"
0635	Reconnaissance plane flying no. 4 line discovers unknown plane 60 miles off the fleet. ??; clear for action
0713	Condition inside the ship: patrol first detainment
0725	Condition inside the ship: patrol second detainment
0853	Full power after one hour
1040	Landing of two fo
1051	Landing of one fo and one fb (situation of the enemy not recognized)
1327	*Zuihō* discovered the periscope of an enemy submarine; clear for action; rudder hard over position to avoid hit
1337	Condition inside the ship: patrol third detainment
1612	Hydrophone recognizes telephone communication in English
1657	Suspicious noises heard in direction 125°; avoiding routing; ready for underwater fighting
1713	Commenced fire to chase off the submarine
1722	Takeoff of one fo
1730	24 knots at once, 30 knots after one hour
1935	Heard suspicious telephone communication from a submarine in direction 222°
2245	Heard suspicious telephone communication from a submarine in direction 205°
October 24: Cloudy	
0530	??
0545	Maximum battle speed immediately
0555	Takeoff of reconnaissance planes (fo × 8); battle meal
0612	Condition inside the ship: patrol first detainment
0638	Destroyer *Akizuki* discovers enemy submarine in direction 220°
0643	Flooding mine discovered in direction 230°
0658	Reconnaissance plane radios "Enemy surface force 207°, 50 miles off Suruan"
0730	Condition inside the ship: patrol second detainment
0805	24 knots at once, maximum battle speed after 30 minutes
0846	Takeoff of one fo × 1 reconnaissance plane
0934	Report received of sighting "0850 250 miles south southwest of own force enemy Mobile Force (4 carriers plus 10 to 20 other ships)"
1020	Clear for action
1025	radio of *Yūgeki-Butai* "Attacked by enemy carrier-based planes"
1020	Takeoff of three fc as CAP
1030	Distribution of battle meal (emergency food)
1045	Condition inside the ship: patrol second detainment
1124	Air attack unit immediate standby condition. Takeoff of four fc as CAP; C-in-C *Yūgeki-Butai* radioed about the fight against 40 enemy planes
1151	Takeoff of the air attack unit (fo × 1, fb × 2, fc × 16, fob × 14)
1224	Landing of fo × 10

1318	Radio of the air attack unit about the fight against enemy fighters
1323	Landing of two fc of the air attack unit, which had developed troubles
1410	Landing of the CAP
1459	Light cruiser *Ōyodo* discovers unknown plane in 250°, 35 km
1510	No. 2 *Guntai* [Force] detainment
1512	Takeoff of four fc as CAP
1520	Takeoff of one fo and one fb
1540	Condition inside the ship: patrol third detainment
1550	Landing of one fb

Notes
Zuikaku's DAR for the remaining hours of October 24 is apparently missing; the next entry refers to the air battles on October 25, even though no date is given.
fo = attack plane; fb = dive-bomber; fc = fighter; CAP = combat air patrol; ASW = antisubmarine warfare

Table 13: DAR, First Air Battle	
Date/Weather/Time Battle sequel (own force) Friendly forces (battle sequel)	
0741	
0749	Air battle (this means battle against the attacking enemy planes)
0800	Immediate standby condition for the CAP (direct protection planes)
0803	
0807	Takeoff of nine fc as CAP
0808	Enemy large unit (approx. 130 aircraft) detected to port 160°, 5° (?) elevation angle, range 6,000 m
0811	Hoisted battle flag
0817	Eleven Grumman dive-bombers approaching at 220°, divided into two groups
0821	Commenced fire
0828	Speed 24 knots
0829	Enemy dive-bombers began the successive dive, and torpedo bombers also began attacking (fb × 40, fo × 10). At starboard 90° to hull side torpedo wake.
0835	Port side at the stern torpedo wake. Portside amidships bomb hit (250 kg).
0837	Torpedo hit no. 4 generator room (flooded completely). List to port 9.5°. Auxiliary control panel, right low-pressure electric-distribution panel, left cable distribution room, no. 10 cable passage, no. 8 cable passage flooded completely. No. 3 foam pump out of action, current source for rudder engine lost, rudder develops troubles. Begin manual steering; after ER to port flooded, impossible to enter and use. Forward ER shaft connection to port destroyed and impossible to use. Owing to heat development, staying in the ER became impossible.
0840	Only the two starboard shafts operable
0845	Flooding of the rapid-counterflooding compartments to correct the list to 6°. Rudder in operation by emergency current source.
0848	All transmitters out of operation
0850	Fire in the no. 2 (section) of the upper and lower hangars. Eight enemy planes attack from starboard 20°.
0854	Fire in the no. 2 (section) of the upper and lower hangars under control
0854	Air battle
0859	Standby condition for gunners
0923	Radio to light cruiser *Ōyodo*: "Inform your communication power!"
0927	??
0940	*Ōyodo* recognizes planes in 180°
0941	*Zuihō* recognizes planes in 280°
0942	*Ōyodo* & *Chitose* recognize planes in 300.°
0950	Transport of shells to the ammunition magazine to starboard from the aft magazine

Table 14: DAR, Second Air Battle	
Date/Weather/Time Battle sequel (own force) Friendly forces (battle sequel)	
0953	Large formation of enemy planes (approx. 30 aircraft) approaching port side 160° (Curtiss fb 14 planes). Air battle, full power ahead.
0958	Commences fire against the planes attacking this ship (fb × 10; fo × 6–8). Two torpedo wakes near the stern to starboard.
1008	Cessation of fire; attack repelled by driving back all enemy planes
1022	Unidentified planes discovered (one Curtiss and one Grumman?)
1033	Flagship changed to *Ōyodo* from *Zuikaku*

1045	Starboard 90°, sighted possible submarine
1051	C-in-C boarded ship's boat
1055	Ahead original speed
1100	Admiral's flag hoisted on ōyodo
1102	Discovered planes between clouds; air battle; full power ahead; commences fire
1104	Starboard 70°, Curtiss fb × 4 discovered
1120	Cessation of fire
1145	Speed 18 knots
1150	Full power ahead, air battle *Ise* discovered in 240°
1158	Battle emergency meal distribution. Destroyer *Hatsuzuki* picks up eight pilots of the CAP commanded by Lt. Kobayashi. Claim to have shot down Grumman fc × 6, fb × 3.
1209	Speed 30 knots
1246	One plane starboard 15°
1248	Air battle
1250	Commences fire
1255	Cessation of fire
1302	
1305	Large group of planes (more than 100 aircraft) approaching port side 160°, elevation angle 4°, range 40,000 m

Table 15: DAR, Third Air Battle

Date/Weather/Time Battle sequel (own force) Friendly forces (battle sequel)	
1306	Air battle. Approaching enemy planes fb × 70, fo 8–11, *Hatsuzuki* approached by enemy planes from fore and aft
1309	Commences fire, speed 24 knots
1321	Torpedo hit port side, list increased to 14° by torpedo and bomb hits, several near misses
1323	Engines and rudder damaged, inoperable; list increased to 20°
1325	Cessation of fire. Flooding and flooded compartments, fierce fires started, no countermeasures possible.
1327	All hands on the flight deck
1328	Commences fire
1330	Photo of the emperor on bridge
1337	Cessation of fire
1339	Commences fire
1342	Cessation of fire
1358	Warship flag stricken, all hands abandon ship, list 23°
1414	Sunk in position 19°57'N, 126°34'E

Note

Robert J. Cressman, in *The Official Chronology of the US Navy in World War II*, p. 267, gives the position as 19°20'N, 125°51'E (220 miles east-northeast of Cape Engaño).

Gun Groups

Fire commenced on the four dive-bombers attacking from the bow direction, then changed to the three bombers diving from the port side 100° and the eight torpedo bombers approaching from port 120°. During the defense firing, one torpedo hit to port aft and caused a breakdown of the electric communications between the fire control system and the gun side, forcing the gunners to aim from the gun side. The sponson of the no. 8 high-angle gun was bent and received a hole, so that the gun was no longer operable; the ammunition hoist was destroyed. No. 5 ammunition magazine was flooded. The supply of ammunition was impossible; no. 2 gun group supplied sixty shells and prepared for the next battle.

Machine Guns

All machine guns to starboard fired upon the fifteen bombers diving from starboard 130°. The machine guns on the port side directed the fire upon the five planes approaching the bow from port. The electronic communications to No. 1, No. 3, and No. 5 Groups broke down, therefore targeting from the gun side. After that, the commanders of the machine gun groups fired independently upon six dive-bombers attacking from starboard and four torpedo planes approaching from port, then ten dive-bombers to port and eight torpedo planes on the same side and five dive-bombers to starboard.

Zuikaku off Cape Engaño early on October 25, 1944. The type 21 radar on top of the island structure can be made out. When the battle commenced, *Zuikaku* had an air complement of twenty-eight A6M5 "Zeke" fighters, sixteen A6M fighter-bombers, seven D4Y2 "Judy" reconnaissance planes, and fourteen "Jill" B6N2 torpedo bombers; sixty-five planes in all.

A photo probably from a 16 mm film taken early on October 25, 1944. The camouflage scheme applied to her hull sides is clearly visible, as is a deck load of airplanes. This is probably the last photo of *Zuikaku* in undamaged condition.

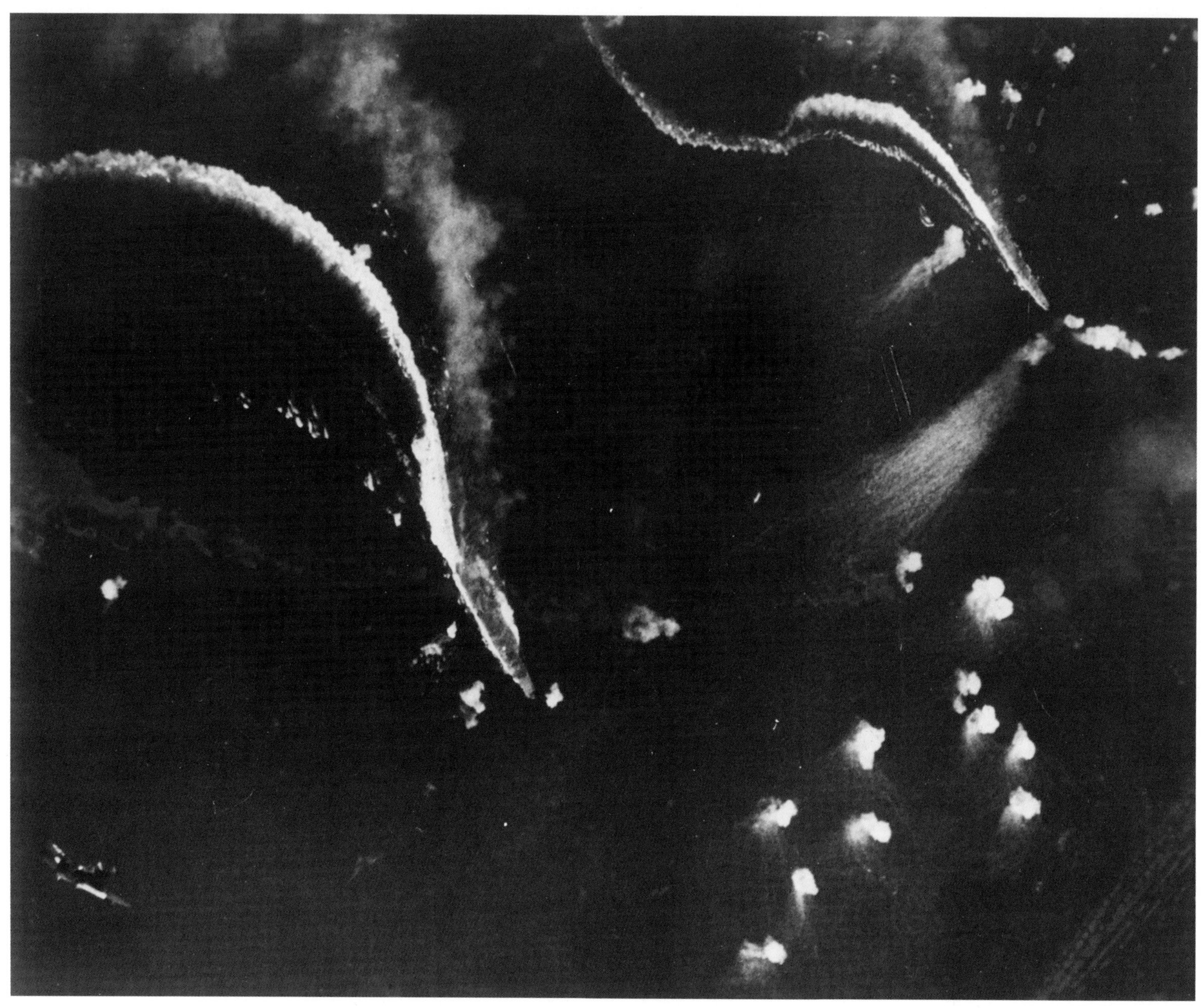

Zuikaku (*left*) and probably the aircraft carrier *Zuihō* (*right*) under attack by US Navy dive-bombers during the Battle off Cape Engaño on October 25, 1944. Both ships appear to make good speed, and this indicates that it is early in the action. Both carriers are emitting heavy smoke. Note the heavy concentration of antiaircraft shell bursts at the lower right and right, and a US Navy Curtiss SB2C Helldiver diving at the lower left. *US Navy*

Zuikaku during her final battle on October 25, 1944, off Cape Engaño. *Zuikaku* was hit by three bombs and one torpedo at about 08:35. Fires broke out, and flooding caused a list to port of 29.5°. About fifteen minutes later the fires had been extinguished, and the list reduced to 6°. Beyond *Zuikaku* is the small aircraft carrier *Zuihō*, and in the foreground the antiaircraft destroyer *Wakatsuki*. *Zuihō* appears to be down by the stern, and *Zuikaku* also appears to be damaged. However, much of the visible smoke was from the firing of the antiaircraft guns and the 12 cm rockets. Of these ships, only *Wakatsuki* would survive. *US Navy*

From the listing flight deck of *Zuikaku* is seen the light cruiser *Oyodo*. This photo was taken by Takeuchi Kōichi, a member of the navy news team, aboard *Zuikaku* just after 10:20 on October 25, 1944, during the Battle of Cape Engaño. About ten minutes later, *Oyodo* came alongside to port, and Vice Admiral Ozawa Jisaburō and his staff were transferred by boat. At 11:00 the vice admiral's flag was hoisted on *Oyodo*. *Kure Maritime Museum*

A photo of *Zuikaku* off Cape Engaño on October 25, 1944. Beginning soon after 13:09, a very large air attack by US carrier planes began, and *Zuikaku* was hit by at least six torpedoes (two to starboard and four to port) and four bombs. The damage caused by these was catastrophic, and flooding increased the port list to 20°, and soon the ship was dead in the water. In this photo the forward elevator appears to be damaged and unusable, and the speed is estimated to be 15–18 knots. Despite the huge clouds of black smoke emitted by the two funnels, their downward-angled configuration kept the flight deck clear of hot gases. Note the camouflaged flight deck. *US Navy*

Zuikaku in sinking condition off Cape Engaño. A US TBM Avenger torpedo bomber is passing the battle area. This photo was probably taken around 13:30, when the list had increased from 14° to 20° and the ship was no longer able to move. *US Navy*

As a result of the second attack, which commenced at about 13:09 and finished at about 13:25, *Zuikaku* had a port list of about 20° and the propulsion system as well as the steering system was inoperable. With the ship crippled, antiaircraft ammunition had to be moved up manually from the magazines below.

At 13:27 the order was given for all hands to assemble on the flight deck. Rear Admiral (he had been promoted on October 15, 1944) Kaizuka Takeo addresses the crew, and all hands salute the lowering of the flag (the photo). Abandon ship was ordered at 13:58, when the list had reached 23°, and at 14:14 she rolled over to port and went down stern first. The survivors were picked up by the destroyers *Wakatsuki and Kuwa.*

Endnotes

Chapter 1

1. *Shō Ichi Gō Sakusen* ("Operation Victory Number 1").

2. Similar to with the other navies designing and building aircraft carriers, the designs of the IJN's first four carriers marked the trial-and-error period of this warship type, which ended with the basic structures decided on and applied in the construction of *Sōryū*. In company with this, the Navy Technical Department, toward the end of 1933, issued "Guidelines for aviation facilities on the aircraft carriers" (as draft) in an effort to regulate the design and the construction of (future) aircraft carriers. However, they were only partly applied, fearing a negative influence on the technical progress. The guidelines are printed as enclosure to Fukui Shizuo's *Kaigun Kantei-shi* ("Japanese naval vessels illustrated, 1869–1945," vol. 3, "Aircraft carriers, seaplane tenders and torpedo boat and submarine tenders") and when reading them the impression is that the fear was not unfounded, but generally speaking, main items can be recognized even in aircraft carriers built during the Pacific War.

3. It must be kept in mind that only the US Navy and the IJN developed carrier-borne aircraft as a main attack weapon for the principal and most other battles in the Pacific War.

4. The Third Naval Armament Replenishment Program of 1937.

5. *Senshi Sōsho* (Tokyo: Bōeichō Bōeikenshūjo Senshibu, 1966–80), vol. 31, pp. 108–75.

Chapter 2

6. The initial requirement had been ninety-six aircraft; namely, twelve type 96 fighters ("Claude"), twenty-four type 96 bombers ("Susie"), twenty-four type 97 attack planes (C3N—construction halted), twelve type 97 reconnaissance aircraft, and twenty-four reserve aircraft of various types. The total of ninety-six aircraft reflected very closely the air complements of *Akagi* and *Kaga* after conversion. An air group on a par with the latter carriers had been perhaps the most important requirement of the Naval General Staff. However, the capacity was limited to a total of eighty-four aircraft by the appearance of new and larger aircraft types and the requirement for the reserve planes; that is, item (2) above.

Chapter 3

7. Two aircraft touched the bridge with their wings after landing, and one plane went overboard.

8 In contrast to *Shōkaku*'s ad hoc arrangements in the upper part of the hull, Kawasaki Kōbe was able to devise a more complete solution because *Zuikaku*'s construction was not so far advanced at the time of the decision.

Chapter 5

9. According to Report S-01-3 of the US Naval Technical Mission to Japan (USNTMtJ), "Surface Warship Hull Design," p. 44, there existed no definitive criteria for roll, pitch, and wind and snow loads as the basis for the design of the flight deck supporting structure; experience and judgment were the determining factors.

10. In *The Maru Special*, no. 6, an example of *Zuikaku* is given, according to which the maximum angle of heel was 40° when sailing in a typhoon with a wind speed of 50 m/sec. The ratio between the lateral areas above (wind pressure) and below the waterline wetted was 1.69.

11. The height of freeboard at the bow was greater than in *Hiryū*. After the experiences with *Ryūjō* and *Sōryū*, the height was now sufficient, in combination with the marked flare of the hull sides, to ensure a dry anchor deck. Speed and reserve buoyancy

were also factors in choice of the height of freeboard; height was the maximum possible when taking into account stability, wind pressure area, and air resistance. This is expressed by the depth/draft ratio, which was 2.59.

12. Data about riveting are omitted.

Chapter 6

13. According to data published by Fukuda Keiji, 9 kg of explosive was detonated 1.52 m below the water surface against models with and without a water layer of various widths and in distances 600–1,400 mm from the hull. The conclusion was that with a water layer depth of 202 mm, the thickness of the protective bulkhead could be reduced by about 50%. It may be of interest to add that the Navy Technical Research Institute (NTRI) tested water layers in 1922 and conducted tests using the multilayer underwater protection system of US battleships of the Colorado class in 1923, but according to *Shōwa Zōsenshi*, p. 657, "They were not so evaluated." However, the effect was reevaluated in the course of the design of the *Kongō* replacement ship and the results of systematic model experiments with small- (NTRI) and medium-sized models (Yokosuka Navy Yard), using 200 kg and 400 kg of explosive. This resulted in the conclusion that in the case of 400 kg of explosive, a 600 mm thick water layer—in contact with the principal protective bulkhead and an empty compartment (air) of a depth of 2,400 mm or more between the outer plate and the water layer—had maximum defensive power. Without a water layer the resistance was reduced to about 100 kg of explosive (!). But this conclusion was drawn in early 1941 and was too late for the Shōkaku class.

14. The stated joint efficiency of 53% seems exceptionally low. Since the heavy oil tanks were adjacent to the protective bulkhead, oiltight riveting (4–4.5/d) would normally have been applied. A joint efficiency of 70%–73% was regularly obtained by this method. It is assumed, therefore, that "53" is a misprint and the actual efficiency was in the range of about 70%.

Chapter 7

15. For more details about aviation facilities, see *Sōryū, Hiryū, and Unryū-Class Aircraft Carriers* in this series.

16. For details, see Lars Ahlberg and Hans Lengerer, *Taihō*, vol. 1 (Gdańsk, Poland: AJ-Press, 2004), 63–76; and Hans Lengerer, *Die Flugzeugträger der Kaiserlichen Japanischen Marine und des Heeres*, vol. 1 (Katowice, Poland: Model Hobby, 2019), 79–90.

Chapter 8

17. The only other IJN warship with the same engine power was the carrier *Taihō*. (Hans Lengerer is indebted to the late Dr. Itani Jirō, who obtained a copy of the relevant documentation from the Historical Branch of the JMSDF at his request.)

18. Note that in the table showing rated power and propeller rpm, no fewer than three types of cruise operation are defined.

19. Actual values were diameter, 4,200 mm; pitch, 4,120 mm; pitch ratio, 0.981; boss ratio, 0.226; ratio of developed blade area, 0.772; and projected area, 0.695. The propellers were of the three-bladed ogival type and were of manganese bronze (*Kaigun Zōsen Gijutsu Gaiyō*, 7:1678; and *Shōwa Zōsenshi*, 1:686).

Chapter 12

20. This report and several others have been published in *Kōkū Bokan Sentō Kiroku* (Tokyo: Atene Shobō, 2002).